Hire
THE KIDS

THE PARENTAL GUIDE

JAMES GUY

Hire the Kids: The Parental Guide

Copyright © 2024 James Guy

All rights reserved.

ISBN:979-8-9899395-5-8

Hire the Kids: The Parental Guide

No part of this book may be reproduced, duplicated, or transmitted without direct written permission from the author or the publisher.

Under no circumstances will any blame or legal responsibility be held against the publisher or author for any damages, reparation, or monetary loss due to the information contained within this book, either directly or indirectly. You are responsible for your own choices, actions, and results.

Legal Notice:

This book is copyright-protected and only for personal use. You cannot amend, distribute, sell, use, quote, or paraphrase any part or the content of this book without the consent of the author or publisher.

Disclaimer Notice:

Please note the information contained within this book is for educational and entertainment purposes only. All efforts have been made to present accurate, up-to-date, reliable, and complete information. No warranties of any kind are declared or implied. Readers acknowledge that the author is not engaging in the rendering of legal, financial, medical, or professional advice. The content of this book has been derived from various sources. Please consult a licensed professional before attempting any techniques outlined in this book.

By reading this book, the reader agrees that under no circumstances will the author be held responsible for any losses, direct or indirect, incurred as a result of using the information contained within this book, including, but not limited to, errors, omissions, or inaccuracies.

About the Author: My journey as an entrepreneur has been enriched by the personal experience of hiring my child in my business endeavors. This unique combination of business owner and parent has provided me with a firsthand understanding of the dynamics involved in blending family and business. Practicing the lessons outlined in this book in my own life, I offer insights not just as a professional but as a parent who has navigated these challenges.

Hire the Kids: The Parental Guide

Hire the Kids: The Parental Guide

Table of Contents

CHAPTER 1: Leveraging Your Child's Potential 1
CHAPTER 2: Financial Favorability 5
    The Freedom of No Financial Burden 7
    The Power of Early Investments 8
    A Generation's Unique Perspective 9
    The Role of Inspirational Figures 10
CHAPTER 3: Shifting the Economic Future 13
    What is the "Rich Kid vs. Poor Kid" Paradigm? 13
    Rich Kid vs. Poor Kid – Real-World Implications 17
    The Path to Financial Literacy and Independence 23
CHAPTER 4: The "Rich Kid" vs "Everybody" 27
    Understanding the "Rich Kid" Attributes 27
    Deconstructing the "Poor Kid" Attributes 29
    The Superior Financial Path of the Rich Kid 35
CHAPTER 5: Building Wealth and Legacy 37
    Tax-Free Wages from Family Businesses 37
    Delayed Gratification and Budgeting Skills 39
    Early Investment in Retirement Accounts 40
    Developing Entrepreneurial Skills Through Work 41
CHAPTER 6: A Parent's Guide to the "Rich Kid" Model 45
    Section 1: Child Labor Laws and Regulations 45
    Section 2: Compensation and Accountability 51
    Section 3: Taxation and Documentation 57
    Section 4: Bookkeepers and Tracking Labor Costs 65
    Section 5: The Significance of Job Descriptions 73
    Section 6: The Zero-Based Budget Approach 77

Hire the Kids: The Parental Guide

Section 7: Your CPA and Hiring Your Child 81

CHAPTER 7: Reinforcing the Rich Kid Model 85

The Benefits of Raising a "Rich Kid" 87

Measuring the "Rich Kid" Model for Your Child 91

Wearing Two Hats: Being Both Parent and Boss 93

Keep Learning: Building a Growth Mindset 94

Why Hiring Your Kid is the Best Move 96

Hire the Kids: The Parental Guide

CHAPTER 1: Leveraging Your Child's Potential

Hiring your children and involving them in your small business from a young age is not only a strategic move for your business but also a tremendous opportunity for your children's personal and financial development. By integrating them into your business operations, you can leverage their natural advantages, setting them up for a future of wealth, success, and entrepreneurial achievement.

Children today are growing up with an innate familiarity with the latest tools and platforms. They understand and use technology intuitively, a skill that took many of us time and effort to acquire. This tech-savvy nature can be a significant asset to your business, helping you implement and adapt to new technologies and cultural trends quickly and efficiently. Their ability to navigate social media, understand data analytics, and apply cutting-edge software can transform your business operations, making them more efficient and forward-thinking. Additionally, their insights into current cultural movements can keep your business relevant and appealing to younger demographics, which is crucial in today's fast-paced market.

One of the greatest advantages of involving your children in your business is their ability to become early adopters of emerging trends. Young people have a keen eye for spotting opportunities as they arise, often before they become widely recognized. This timely engagement can yield substantial benefits, as being first to market can provide a significant competitive edge. Encouraging your children to explore and invest in these opportunities nurtures their entrepreneurial spirit and teaches them valuable lessons about risk and reward. This proactive approach positions them to achieve significant financial growth and build a foundation for long-term wealth. They learn to recognize potential, assess risks, and take calculated steps to capitalize on new trends.

Young individuals are generally more open to experimenting with and embracing new ideas. They are not bound by traditional methods or established routines, making them more flexible and

Hire the Kids: The Parental Guide

innovative. This willingness to try new approaches and learn from failures is invaluable in driving your business forward. Fresh perspectives and a readiness to question the status quo can lead to breakthroughs that set your business apart from the competition. This flexibility enables them to adapt quickly and capitalize on disruptive innovations, positioning them advantageously in the evolving market landscape.

Children also have extensive social networks, especially through digital platforms, offering a powerful avenue for business growth. Their ability to influence and drive trends within their peer groups can rapidly accelerate the adoption of new products, services, or ideas. Leveraging their social networks can create momentum for your business initiatives, leading to increased visibility and demand. Their understanding of digital marketing, social media strategies, and influencer dynamics provides valuable insights into reaching younger audiences, crafting targeted campaigns, engaging with online communities, and building brand loyalty among new demographics.

Another major benefit is that children can learn about financial planning and investment strategies from a young age. By starting early, they can harness the power of compounding interest, which allows their investments to grow exponentially over time. Small amounts saved and invested today can multiply many times over, setting the stage for substantial financial growth. This early start in financial education teaches them the importance of saving, investing, and the disciplined management of money.

Involving children in your business can help them develop problem-solving, critical thinking, and effective communication skills. They gain firsthand experience in handling various aspects of the business, from customer service to marketing to financial management. This wide-ranging exposure equips them with a diverse skill set that is highly valuable in any professional setting. It also fosters a sense of responsibility and ownership, encouraging them to take initiative and make informed decisions.

Parents can get excited about the potential their children have to become successful entrepreneurs and business leaders. By providing

Hire the Kids: The Parental Guide

them with the opportunity to participate in the family business, parents are giving their children a head start in the world of business. They are not only preparing them for future success but also instilling in them the values of hard work, innovation, and financial literacy. This hands-on experience is invaluable and cannot be replicated in a classroom setting.

Children who actively participate in the family business are more likely to develop a strong work ethic and a deep understanding of what it takes to run a successful enterprise. They gain insights into the challenges and rewards of entrepreneurship, which will serve them well throughout their careers. This practical knowledge, combined with their natural, technological prowess and innovative mindset, positions them to excel in the modern economy.

Furthermore, involving children in the business fosters a sense of connection and continuity within the family. It strengthens family bonds and creates a shared sense of purpose, as everyone works together towards common goals. This collaborative environment helps children feel valued and appreciated, boosting their confidence and self-esteem. It also provides them with a support system that encourages their growth and development.

In summary, hiring your children and involving them in the family business offers numerous benefits that extend beyond immediate business gains. It equips them with the skills, knowledge, and mindset needed to navigate the complexities of the modern economy, setting them on a path to financial independence and entrepreneurial success. By leveraging their familiarity with technology and culture, encouraging early adoption of trends, fostering a willingness to embrace new ideas, and capitalizing on their extensive peer networks, parents can give their children a significant head start in life. This approach not only benefits the business but also ensures that the next generation is well-prepared to carry forward the legacy of innovation, resilience, and financial acumen.

Hire the Kids: The Parental Guide

Hire the Kids: The Parental Guide

CHAPTER 2: Financial Favorability

When young people get a head start with financial education, it opens incredible opportunities for growth, innovation, and success. Kids have unique advantages over adults in this area, advantages that can steer them toward financial independence and entrepreneurial success much earlier than might be expected.

For parents who are eager to harness the unique advantages of their children's youth, this guide lays the groundwork for a prosperous future, a golden opportunity for growth, innovation, and success. Unlike adults, children have a distinct set of advantages that, when nurtured, can set them on a path to financial independence and entrepreneurial achievement.

There are four financial favorability traits that children inherently have over their parents: They don't have any financial burdens in the form of debt from past purchases, they can invest early and get compounding to work in their favor for future finances, they can recognize movements and take advantage of the culture shifts in today's trends, and they can call upon the assistance of wise and experienced mentors much sooner in life to guide them towards perpetual progress when they have questions.

All kids have these inherent advantages, and they can be cultivated and directed toward achieving financial success and innovation. By understanding and leveraging these four financially favorable fundamental elements, parents can equip their children with the tools, knowledge, and mindset needed to navigate the complexities of the modern financial world.

ALL KIDS

PAST PURCHASES	FUTURE FINANCES
• No Debt Accumulation from previous purchases • Most of their Income could be considered Disposable	• Early Investing Compounds Interest on earnings over time • Early Reinvestment of Dividends Increase Returns over time
TODAY'S TRENDS	**PERPETUAL PROGRESS**
• Touchstone events and shared experiences shape the culture and create Generational Trends	• Exposure, Mentorship, and Imagination produce endless opportunities to create new solutions

FINANCIAL FAVORABILITIES

Hire the Kids: The Parental Guide

The Freedom of No Financial Burden

One of the most significant advantages that children possess is their freedom from financial burdens. Unlike adults, who often navigate a complex web of financial responsibilities, including mortgages, loans, and daily expenses, children are not directly responsible for such obligations. This unique position provides an opportunity to build a strong financial foundation. By recognizing and appreciating this freedom, parents can guide their children to make wise financial decisions from an early age, free from the constraints that accompany adult financial responsibilities.

However, if you don't educate your kids on how to recognize the debt pitfalls, they can easily fall into early debt accumulation. One of the most common scenarios is the pursuit of higher education, which, without scholarships, financial aid, or proper planning, can saddle students with significant student loan debt upon graduation. Additionally, the allure of credit cards presents a strong temptation for those stepping into financial independence. Without a solid understanding of how interest rates and minimum payments work, credit card debt can quickly become overwhelming. The purchase of a first car also introduces the potential for debt, as high interest rates and long-term loans for expensive vehicles can impose financial strains. Furthermore, as young adults begin earning their first paychecks, there's a tendency to increase spending on lifestyle upgrades, a phenomenon known as lifestyle inflation. This can lead to a cycle of living paycheck to paycheck, relying on credit, and accumulating debt to maintain a certain standard of living.

To preserve a clean financial slate for your children, start by teaching them key strategies about budgeting, saving, investing, and the responsible use of credit. This prepares young adults with the knowledge to make informed financial decisions. Practicing living within one's means—spending less than what is earned and saving the difference—is a vital habit that can help avoid lifestyle inflation and unnecessary debt accumulation. When borrowing becomes necessary, it's important to understand the terms and conditions of loans and credit, seek the best interest rates, and only borrow what

Hire the Kids: The Parental Guide

is absolutely needed to prevent overwhelming debt. Starting financial planning early, including setting money aside for education, major purchases, and emergencies, can significantly reduce the need to go into debt for these expenses, laying the groundwork for a financially secure future free from the burdens of debt.

The financial safety net provided by parents plays an important role in the early financial lives of children, especially when it comes to covering basic needs such as food, shelter, clothing, and education. This foundational support allows kids to approach their own income with a degree of flexibility and strategy that is often unavailable to their peers without such a safety net.

By meeting these fundamental requirements, parents not only ensure the well-being and security of their children but also afford them the opportunity to use their personal income in ways that can further their financial growth and independence. Instead of allocating their earnings towards living expenses, children can contribute to savings, explore investment opportunities, or even fund their entrepreneurial ventures at a very young age. This strategic use of income, enabled by parental support, lays the groundwork for a solid financial future, emphasizing the importance of saving and investing over mere consumption.

Furthermore, this setup introduces children to the concept of financial planning and prioritization early on. They learn to distinguish between needs and wants, a skill that is invaluable in managing finances effectively throughout life. With their basic needs secured, kids have the luxury of planning long-term, whether it's saving for college, investing in stocks, or starting a savings account that benefits from compound interest over time.

The Power of Early Investments

The adage "time is money" holds profound implications for the young. Children have the extraordinary advantage of time, which, when paired with early financial investments, can leverage the magic of compounding interest. Even small amounts invested early in life can grow into significant sums over the decades, thanks to the

Hire the Kids: The Parental Guide

compounding effect. Compounding, often described as interest on interest, means that the initial investment grows not just from the original amount but also from the accumulated interest over time. This effect becomes more potent over longer durations, making early childhood and adolescence the optimal times to begin investing.

With decades ahead before retirement or other financial goals, young investors have the unique opportunity to see their investments grow exponentially. A small amount saved and invested today can multiply many times over, thanks to the compounding effect. For example, if a child starts investing just a small amount monthly at the age of 10, by the time they reach their 60s, the investment could have grown significantly, assuming a reasonable average annual return. Early starters can achieve substantial financial growth with relatively lower initial investments compared to those who start investing later in life. This means that children who begin investing their money can build considerable wealth over time, even if they invest smaller amounts but consistently.

Starting early also allows for a higher risk tolerance in investment choices. Young investors have the time to recover from market fluctuations and learn from their investment decisions without jeopardizing their long-term financial goals. This learning curve is invaluable, as it provides real-world experience in financial markets, helping them make more informed decisions as they grow older.

The practice of investing from a young age instills a savings and investment mindset. Young investors learn the value of money, the importance of financial planning, and the discipline of saving for the future. This mentality is necessary for maintaining financial health and achieving long-term financial goals.

A Generation's Unique Perspective

Every generation is influenced by its economic, technological, and cultural environment, shaping its perspective and opportunities. Today's children are growing up in a world that is vastly different from that of their parents, with unprecedented access to

Hire the Kids: The Parental Guide

information, technology, and global networks. This unique vantage point equips them with the potential to identify and capitalize on opportunities that their parents might not see. If our kids can be taught to leverage this generational perspective, it can open doors to new avenues of financial and entrepreneurial success.

The extended investment horizon that kids enjoy inherently allows for a more aggressive approach to investing, including the adoption of riskier, potentially higher-reward investment strategies. This long timeframe before the need for withdrawal, such as for retirement or significant life events, affords children the unique advantage of weathering the market's inherent volatility, experimenting with different investment vehicles, and learning from these experiences without jeopardizing their long-term financial stability.

One of the fundamental principles of investing is the risk-return trade-off, which posits that higher returns are associated with higher risk. Kids, with their long investment horizon, can afford to allocate a portion of their portfolio to riskier assets such as stocks, which, despite their volatility, historically offer higher returns over the long term compared to more conservative investments like bonds or savings accounts. The ability to ride out the short-term fluctuations of the market without needing to liquidate positions for immediate cash needs is a luxury that time affords young investors.

The Role of Inspirational Figures

Parents, teachers, and role models play a pivotal role in inspiring the entrepreneurial spirit and imagination in children. The stories, lessons, and values imparted by these figures lay the groundwork for a mindset that seeks to solve modern-day problems with innovative solutions. When parents emphasize the importance of surrounding their children with positive influences, it encourages creative thinking and fosters an environment where entrepreneurial ideas are promoted and celebrated.

Technology fosters creativity and innovation; children with access to the internet and digital devices can access vast amounts of information instantly. This allows them to learn about diverse

Hire the Kids: The Parental Guide

cultures, global issues, and scientific advancements. Social media platforms are another technological force shaping the current generation's perspective. These platforms connect children globally, allowing them to share ideas, experiences, and opinions. This connectivity breaks down geographical barriers, fostering a sense of global citizenship and collective awareness. Children are exposed to a multitude of viewpoints, which can enhance their understanding of complex international issues and promote empathy and cultural awareness.

Hire the Kids: The Parental Guide

Hire the Kids: The Parental Guide

CHAPTER 3: Shifting the Economic Future

The lessons we teach our children about money, work, and entrepreneurship can significantly shape their future. Hiring your child to work in your small business opens a transformative educational pathway, diverging sharply from traditional notions of child allowances and part-time jobs. The "Rich Kid vs. Poor Kid" model introduces an enlightening perspective by illustrating two distinct paths children might follow based on their early financial education and opportunities.

Early involvement in business operations can significantly impact a child's financial literacy and entrepreneurial mindset. To effectively involve your children in your business, start by assigning age-appropriate tasks that align with their interests and skills. The "Rich Kid vs. Poor Kid" paradigm underscores the long-term benefits of early financial education and active participation in economic activities, setting the stage for a prosperous and responsible future.

What is the "Rich Kid vs. Poor Kid" Paradigm?

The narrative of "Rich Kid vs. Poor Kid" is not a straightforward tale of affluence versus poverty but rather a discussion of the richness of financial knowledge and entrepreneurial spirit versus the poverty of economic ignorance and passivity. It prompts a reevaluation of our approach to teaching children about money. Central to this narrative is the comparison between two paradigms: one where children are engaged in their family's economic activities, gaining firsthand experience in income generation, money management, investment, and skill development, and another where children are more removed from these experiences, often receiving money passively as an allowance, with a focus on consumption and the potential development of a dependency on external financial sources.

The "Rich Kid" is immersed in an environment where financial education is a part of everyday life. These children see their parents or guardians working, making financial decisions, and dealing with

Hire the Kids: The Parental Guide

the ups and downs of business ownership. They learn through observation and participation, understanding that money is earned through effort, innovation, and risk-taking. This hands-on experience teaches them the value of hard work and instills a sense of responsibility and independence. They learn to appreciate the effort behind earning money and develop a respect for its value. By being involved in the family business, they gain practical skills that should be taught in schools, such as budgeting, investing, and negotiating.

In contrast, the "Poor Kid" in this context might receive money without understanding the effort required to earn it. Their experience with money is often limited to spending allowances given by parents, which can foster a mindset of dependency and entitlement. The absence of the chance to participate in economic activities means that these children could potentially lose valuable opportunities to learn about financial responsibility, the significance of saving, and the fundamentals of investing. They might view money as a means to an end, primarily for consumption, rather than a tool for creating opportunities and building wealth. This can result in a lack of understanding about finances and being ready for future economic challenges.

Involving children in a family business or economic activities provides them with a practical education that goes beyond theoretical knowledge. They learn to manage their own money, make investment decisions, and understand the consequences of financial choices. This experience can foster an entrepreneurial spirit, encouraging them to think creatively and take initiative. They see firsthand how businesses operate, the challenges involved, and the strategies needed for success. This prepares them for future entrepreneurial endeavors and equips them with the necessary skills to navigate the complexities of the modern economy.

Moreover, children involved in family businesses often develop a strong work ethic and a sense of responsibility. They understand that their actions have direct consequences on the business and, by extension, the family's financial well-being. This sense of accountability can drive them to work harder, be more disciplined,

Hire the Kids: The Parental Guide

and strive for excellence. They learn the importance of perseverance, resilience, and adaptability—qualities that are essential for success in any field.

On the other hand, children who are not exposed to such experiences might need to develop these skills and qualities. They might lack the motivation to work hard or take risks as they do not see the direct benefits of doing so. Without the experience of managing money and making financial decisions, they might struggle with financial independence in adulthood. They might find it challenging to budget, save, or invest wisely, which can limit their financial growth and opportunities.

The dichotomy between the 'Rich Kid' and the 'Poor Kid' is not solely about financial status but about the learning and growth opportunities each child is exposed to. Involving children in economic activities can help bridge the gap and provide them with the necessary tools to thrive. It's important to teach them that wealth is not just about having money but about possessing the knowledge and skills to manage and grow it. We can instill in them the values of hard work, responsibility, and independence, paving the way for their long-term financial success. This transformative approach, as illustrated by the 'Rich Kid vs. Poor Kid' narrative, can reshape the way children perceive and handle money, preparing them for a future of financial security and success. Let this narrative inspire us to revolutionize financial education.

In essence, the "Rich Kid vs. Poor Kid" narrative encourages us to rethink our approach to financial education. It highlights the importance of practical, hands-on learning experiences in shaping a child's financial future. By engaging children in the family's economic activities, we can provide them with a solid foundation of financial knowledge and skills. We can foster an entrepreneurial spirit, a strong work ethic, and a sense of responsibility. We can assist them in cultivating a positive relationship with money, recognizing it not merely as a tool for consumption but as a powerful instrument for creating opportunities and amassing wealth.

Hire the Kids: The Parental Guide

This approach has the potential to revolutionize children's financial perspectives, equipping them for a future of economic security and success. It empowers them to steer their financial destiny, make informed decisions, and pursue their entrepreneurial aspirations. Ultimately, it can help them evolve into not just 'Rich Kids' in terms of wealth but rich in knowledge, skills, and opportunities, ensuring a financially secure and independent future.

Hire the Kids: The Parental Guide

Rich Kid vs. Poor Kid – Real-World Implications

The story of "Rich Kid vs. Poor Kid" goes beyond mere financial status and delves into the richness of financial knowledge and entrepreneurial spirit versus the poverty of economic ignorance and passivity. It highlights how different approaches to money and work can shape a child's understanding of value, responsibility, and future opportunities. It's important to recognize that no child is entirely a "Rich Kid" or a "Poor Kid." Instead, all children fall somewhere on the spectrum, influenced by their environments and experiences. For parents with a small business or side hustle, involving your children in your business can significantly increase their chances of adopting the beneficial practices associated with being a Rich Kid.

In the real world, these differences can present themselves in various ways. A Rich Kid earns tax-free income by working within the family business and learns the direct correlation between effort and reward. This experience instills a sense of responsibility and a deeper appreciation for the money they earn. In contrast, a Poor Kid might receive sporadic allowances or gifts without a direct link to their efforts, leading to a limited understanding of money's true value and the effort required to earn it.

Rich Kids are also taught the importance of delayed gratification. By managing their earnings through structured bank accounts and zero-based budgets, they learn financial discipline early on. This contrasts with Poor Kids, who are often raised as immediate consumers and encouraged to spend their money on instant gratifications. This habit fosters a short-term financial outlook, making it harder for them to develop economic independence and stability.

Investment opportunities are another significant differentiator. Rich Kids have the advantage of starting to invest early, with options like putting money into an Individual Retirement Account (IRA) as soon as they start earning a wage. This early start teaches them the importance of saving for the future and the power of compound interest, setting them up for long-term financial growth. In contrast, Poor Kids might not have the same opportunities or encouragement

Hire the Kids: The Parental Guide

to invest, potentially leading them to rely on credit cards or other forms of debt, creating a cycle of dependency.

Skill development and entrepreneurship are crucial aspects of the Rich Kid experience. By being involved in their family's business, they gain exposure to business operations, innovation, and critical thinking. These skills are absolutely invaluable and will certainly lead to a profound understanding of how businesses function and how to navigate the complexities of the entrepreneurial world. Poor Kids, on the other hand, might not receive the same level of exposure to these experiences, focusing instead on recreational activities and education without a balanced view of financial growth and asset accumulation.

Parents with small businesses or side hustles have a unique opportunity to bridge this gap. By hiring their children and involving them in the industry, they can provide real-world experiences that teach valuable financial lessons. Children can gain knowledge about income generation, financial discipline, investment strategies, and entrepreneurial skills. These experiences play a pivotal role in fostering a robust work ethic, instilling an appreciation for the value of money, and cultivating the capacity to make well-informed financial decisions.

For instance, when children are hired to work in the family business, they see firsthand the effort and dedication required to run a successful enterprise. They learn the importance of showing up on time, completing tasks, and contributing to the team's success. This experience teaches them responsibility and the value of hard work, traits that are crucial for future success.

Moreover, involving children in financial discussions and decisions can enhance their understanding of money management. By seeing how budgeting, saving, and investing are done in a real-world context, they gain practical knowledge that goes beyond theoretical concepts taught in schools. This hands-on learning helps them understand the importance of financial planning and the long-term benefits of wise financial choices.

Hire the Kids: The Parental Guide

Encouraging children to invest their earnings early can have profound effects on their financial future. By opening an IRA or other investment accounts, they can start to see the benefits of compound interest. This not only teaches them about the power of investing but also instills a habit of saving and planning for the future.

Skill development and entrepreneurial spirit are further nurtured when children are given responsibilities within the family business. Whether it's managing a small project, helping with marketing, or assisting with customer service, these tasks provide them with practical skills that are highly valuable in any career. They learn to think critically, solve problems, and innovate—skills that will serve them well throughout their lives.

Ultimately, the goal is not to create a dichotomy where one child is purely a Rich Kid and another purely a Poor Kid but to blend the beneficial practices of the Rich Kid into every child's upbringing. Incorporating children into the family business can provide them with valuable tools, knowledge, and experiences that cultivate financial literacy, independence, and an entrepreneurial mindset. This approach not only benefits the children but also strengthens the family business, creating a legacy of knowledge, resilience, and success that can be passed down through generations.

Hire the Kids: The Parental Guide

RICH KIDS

INCOME	DELAYED GRATIFICATION
• Potential Tax-Free Wages from Parents' Business	• Encouraged to use a Zero-Based Budget to Control Impulses and Reward Patience
INVESTMENT OPPORTUNITIES	**SKILL DEVELOPMENT & ENTREPRENEURSHIP**
• Eligible to contribute to a Roth IRA at an early age	• Unconventional Learning Opportunities

INCOME: In this quadrant, income represents tax-free money earned from working within the parent's business. Unlike a traditional allowance, this income is tied to actual work, instilling a sense of responsibility and value for money earned.

DELAYED GRATIFICATION: For the Rich Kid, this involves learning to manage their earnings through structured bank accounts and zero-based budgets. This approach provides direction and control, fostering financial discipline.

INVESTMENT OPPORTUNITIES: The Rich Kid is positioned to invest, with options like putting money into an Individual Retirement Account (IRA) as soon as they start earning a wage. This early start in investment teaches not only the importance of saving for the future but also the power of compound interest.

Hire the Kids: The Parental Guide

SKILL DEVELOPMENT & ENTREPRENEURSHIP: Rich Kids benefit from skill development and entrepreneurship opportunities by being involved in their family's business. This exposure encourages innovation, critical thinking, and a deep understanding of business operations.

Hire the Kids: The Parental Guide

POOR KIDS

ALLOWANCE	IMMEDIATE CONSUMPTION
• Occasional Money from Chores, Birthday Gifts; Special Occasions	• Encouraged to Indulge in Spontaneous Spending, Neglecting Budget Discipline
CREDIT DEPENDANCY	RECREATION & EDUCATION
• Taxable income from a Non-Family business leading to High-Interest Credit Debt	• Conventional Learning Opportunities

ALLOWANCE: In the Poor Kid quadrant, money often comes sporadically from chores, gifts, or special occasions, not tied to any work performed. This can create a disconnect between effort and reward, limiting the understanding of money's value.

IMMEDIATE CONSUMPTION: Poor Kids are often raised as consumers, encouraged to spend on immediate gratifications rather than saving or investing. This habit fosters a short-term financial outlook, potentially hampering financial independence.

CREDIT DEPENDENCY: Without a tie to a family business or entrepreneurial endeavors, Poor Kids might feel compelled to seek external employment early or rely on credit cards with unfavorable terms, leading to a cycle of dependency and potential debt.

Hire the Kids: The Parental Guide

RECREATION & EDUCATION: In this quadrant, emphasis is placed on spending for recreation and education, often prioritizing consumables and experiences over financial assets. While not inherently negative, this focus might not encourage a balanced view of financial growth and asset accumulation.

The Path to Financial Literacy and Independence

The "Rich Kid vs. Poor Kid" comparison encourages a reevaluation of how we approach teaching children about money, highlighting the importance of engaging them in real-world economic activities. For parents with small businesses or side hustles, involving their children in the family enterprise can significantly influence their financial habits and understanding, fostering attributes that lead to long-term success.

Income vs. Allowance

The distinction between income earned through work and an allowance received without direct effort is crucial in shaping a child's perception of money. Income earned from working in the family business teaches children the value of labor and financial reward, instilling a sense of responsibility and an understanding of money's worth. For instance, a child who helps out with inventory management, customer service, or marketing efforts in the family store learns firsthand the effort required to earn money. They begin to appreciate the relationship between work and financial gain, leading to a more profound respect for the value of money.

Conversely, an allowance given without linking it to work can skew a child's perception of money. When children receive money irregularly from chores, gifts, or special occasions without understanding the effort involved, they may not fully grasp the concept of earning. This can create a disconnect between effort and reward, limiting their understanding of money's true value. For instance, when a child receives a weekly allowance in exchange for minimal household chores, there is a possibility that they may begin to perceive money as readily available. This perception can potentially lead to a lack of financial discipline and foster a sense of entitlement.

Delayed Gratification vs. Immediate Consumption

Learning the importance of delayed gratification is a critical component of effective money management. Rich Kids, who are taught to manage their earnings through structured bank accounts and zero-based budgets, develop financial control and discipline. They learn to set financial goals, save for the future, and make thoughtful spending decisions. For instance, a child who earns money from working in the family business and saves a portion of their earnings for a desired purchase, like a new bike, learns valuable lessons about patience, planning, and the rewards of saving.

In contrast, Poor Kids often adopt a consumption-focused approach, emphasizing immediate spending over saving. When money is received as an allowance or gift without any associated effort, the tendency is to spend it quickly on immediate gratifications, like toys or snacks. This habit fosters a short-term financial outlook, making it harder for them to develop the discipline needed for long-term economic stability. An example of this might be a child who spends their entire allowance as soon as they receive it, without any thought to saving or budgeting for future needs, potentially leading to poor money management skills in adulthood.

Investment Opportunities vs. Credit Dependency

Rich Kids have the advantage of early exposure to investment opportunities, which fosters a mindset of growth and future planning. When children are encouraged to invest their earnings, such as contributing to an Individual Retirement Account (IRA) or other investment vehicles, they learn about the power of compound interest and the benefits of long-term savings. For example, a child who starts investing a portion of their earnings from the family business at a young age will see their money grow significantly over time, teaching them the value of saving and investing for the future.

In contrast, Poor Kids might not have the same opportunities or encouragement to invest, often leading to a reliance on credit.

Hire the Kids: The Parental Guide

Without the financial literacy to understand the implications of debt, these children might resort to using credit cards with unfavorable terms, leading to a cycle of dependency and potential financial insecurity. For instance, a teenager who is not taught about the importance of saving and investing might open a credit card to fund discretionary spending, quickly accruing debt and struggling with high-interest payments, which can hinder their financial independence and stability.

Skill Development & Entrepreneurship vs. Recreation & Education

Involving children in a family business provides invaluable opportunities for skill development and entrepreneurship. Rich Kids benefit from hands-on learning and the chance to innovate, gain a deep understanding of business operations, and develop critical thinking and problem-solving skills. For example, a child involved in the family business might take on responsibilities like managing social media accounts, handling customer inquiries, or assisting with financial planning. These experiences not only enhance their practical skills but also cultivate an entrepreneurial mindset that can be applied to future ventures.

On the other hand, Poor Kids might focus more on recreation and traditional education, which, while valuable, may only sometimes translate into practical financial wisdom or business acumen. Emphasizing consumption and leisure activities over financial growth can limit a child's exposure to real-world economic challenges and opportunities. For instance, a child who spends most of their time on recreational activities and receives money for spending without understanding how to earn or manage it might miss out on learning essential skills that are crucial for future success.

The comparison between Rich Kids and Poor Kids underscores the tangible benefits of integrating children into family businesses. It highlights how early financial experiences and active participation in economic activities can profoundly impact a child's future financial behavior and success. By involving children in the family business, parents can provide a practical education that goes beyond

Hire the Kids: The Parental Guide

theoretical knowledge, instilling values of hard work, financial discipline, and entrepreneurial spirit.

Parents with small businesses or side hustles have a unique opportunity to shape their children's financial futures positively. By hiring their children and involving them in business operations, they can teach valuable lessons about income generation, financial management, investment strategies, and skill development. The experiences play a pivotal role in cultivating a robust work ethic, fostering an appreciation for the value of money, and honing the skill to make well-informed financial decisions. This approach not only ensures the long-term success of the children but also bolsters the family business, establishing a legacy of knowledge, resilience, and financial understanding that can be passed down through generations.

Hire the Kids: The Parental Guide

CHAPTER 4: The "Rich Kid" vs "Everybody"

The Rich Kid vs. Everybody: A Deep Dive into Financial Futures

The concept of the "Rich Kid vs. Everybody" isn't just about comparing children of wealth to those without; it's a framework for understanding the fundamental differences in upbringing, financial education, and long-term opportunities between those who are strategically raised with a focus on earning, saving, and investing, versus those who might be raised in an environment where financial literacy is undervalued or overlooked. This essay explores these contrasts in depth, focusing on the four key attributes that secure the future of the so-called "Rich Kid"—tax-free wages from businesses owned solely by their parents, disciplined spending habits enforced by budgeting, early and strategic investment in retirement accounts, and entrepreneurial skill development through meaningful work experience. We then contrast these with the four traits that contribute to financial uncertainty for the "Poor Kid": unreliable allowances, consumerist tendencies, early credit dependency, and a conventional lifestyle that prioritizes recreation over entrepreneurship.

In this analysis, we will further break down the mindsets, relationships, and circumstances that can create a "Poor Kid" mindset, specifically focusing on the influences of inherited wealth, entitlement, nepotism, and side hustles. By examining how each of these factors can shape a child's financial future, we can better understand why the "Rich Kid" model—focused on earned income, financial literacy, and merit-based success—is superior for preparing children for a stable and prosperous future.

Understanding the "Rich Kid" Attributes

Before we delve into the analysis of what contributes to a 'Poor Kid' mindset, it's crucial to fully comprehend the attributes that define a 'Rich Kid'. These attributes set them up for long-term financial success and form the basis for our comparison.

Hire the Kids: The Parental Guide

Tax-Free Wages from Family Businesses

One of the most significant advantages the Rich Kid has is earning tax-free wages through their involvement in a family-owned business. In the United States, if a child under 18 works for a sole proprietorship owned by their parents, their income is exempt from Social Security and Medicare taxes, provided the earnings remain under the standard deduction amount. This setup allows children to earn money without the typical tax burdens that come with traditional employment, giving them a head start on saving and wealth accumulation.

For example, a child who earns $12,000 in a year working for their parents can save that money entirely, whereas a peer working a part-time job at a local business would see a significant portion of their income deducted for taxes. This tax advantage provides the Rich Kid with more disposable income to save, invest, or use for educational purposes, setting a foundation for financial independence early in life.

Delayed Gratification and Budgeting

Another cornerstone of the Rich Kid model is the emphasis on delayed gratification, often enforced through strict budgeting practices. Children in this model are taught from a young age to manage their money through a zero-based budgeting approach, where every dollar has a specific purpose—whether for savings, investments, or spending. This discipline in managing finances not only curbs impulsive spending but also ingrains the value of money and the importance of financial planning.

In contrast, children who are not exposed to these practices may develop a habit of spending money as soon as they receive it, leading to poor financial habits that can persist into adulthood. The ability to budget effectively is a critical skill that differentiates the Rich Kid from others, as it enables them to prioritize long-term financial goals over short-term pleasures.

Early Investment Opportunities

Hire the Kids: The Parental Guide

One of the most powerful tools for building wealth is time, and the Rich Kid model takes full advantage of this by encouraging early investments in retirement accounts like a Roth IRA. Since contributions to a Roth IRA are made with after-tax dollars, the money grows tax-free, and qualified withdrawals in retirement are also tax-free. Starting a Roth IRA at a young age allows the Rich Kid to benefit from decades of compound interest, potentially leading to significant savings by the time they reach retirement age.

The idea here is simple: the earlier you start investing, the more time your money has to grow. For instance, if a child starts contributing to a Roth IRA at age 15 and continues to contribute $5,000 annually, by the time they reach 65, their account could be worth well over a million dollars, depending on the rate of return. This early investment strategy is a key element of the Rich Kid's financial plan and contrasts sharply with the Poor Kid's approach, where investment opportunities are often delayed or ignored altogether.

Entrepreneurial Skill Development

Working in a family-owned business also provides the Rich Kid with invaluable opportunities to develop entrepreneurial skills. Unlike traditional part-time jobs, where the focus is often on completing tasks without much room for creativity or innovation, working in a family business allows the child to see the inner workings of a business, understand the challenges and rewards of entrepreneurship, and contribute ideas that could shape the future of the business.

This experience fosters critical thinking, problem-solving, and leadership skills, all of which are essential for success in any field. Moreover, by being involved in the family business, the Rich Kid is more likely to develop a strong work ethic and a sense of ownership, which can drive them to pursue their entrepreneurial ventures in the future.

Deconstructing the "Poor Kid" Attributes

While the Rich Kid benefits from strategic financial planning, disciplined spending, and entrepreneurial experience, the Poor Kid

Hire the Kids: The Parental Guide

often faces a very different reality. The Poor Kid's financial future is shaped by unreliable allowances, consumerist tendencies, early credit dependency, and a lifestyle that prioritizes recreation and secular education over entrepreneurship. These factors can significantly hinder their ability to achieve financial stability and independence.

RICH KIDS vs EVERYBODY

INHERITED WEALTH VS EARNED INCOME	ENTITLEMENT VS EMPOWERMENT
NEPOTISM VS MERITOCRACY	SIDE HUSTLES VS TAX-FREE WAGES

The Pitfalls of Inherited Wealth

One of the most misunderstood aspects of wealth is the notion that inheriting money automatically sets a person up for life. While inheriting wealth can provide a financial cushion, it can also create significant challenges, especially for minors. Without proper

Hire the Kids: The Parental Guide

financial education and guidance, a windfall inheritance can quickly spiral out of control.

Statistics show that a large percentage of individuals who inherit wealth end up losing it within a few years. According to a study by The Williams Group, 70% of wealthy families lose their wealth by the second generation, and 90% lose it by the third generation. This phenomenon, often referred to as "shirt sleeves to shirt sleeves in three generations," highlights the dangers of inheriting wealth without the financial literacy to manage it effectively.

For minors, the risks are even greater. A sudden influx of money from an inheritance, lottery winnings, or a legal settlement can lead to impulsive spending, poor financial decisions, and even exploitation by unscrupulous individuals. Without the discipline and financial education that the Rich Kid model emphasizes, a Poor Kid who inherits wealth may lack the skills needed to manage it responsibly, leading to financial ruin.

Additionally, inheritances and windfalls are subject to significant taxation. For example, federal estate taxes can take up to 40% of the value of the estate, depending on the amount. Lottery winnings are taxed as ordinary income, with federal taxes taking a large chunk and state taxes potentially adding to the burden. In contrast, earned income for minors working in a family business is not subject to these taxes if it falls below the standard deduction threshold, giving the Rich Kid a clear advantage in terms of wealth preservation.

The key difference between the Poor Kid who inherits wealth and the Rich Kid who earns it is financial literacy. The Rich Kid learns to manage money, delay gratification, and invest wisely from a young age, whereas the Poor Kid may receive a large sum of money without the skills to manage it effectively. This disparity in financial education can lead to vastly different outcomes, with the Rich Kid more likely to achieve long-term financial stability and success.

The Dangers of Entitlement

Another significant factor that can contribute to a Poor Kid mindset is a sense of entitlement. This often develops in situations where a

Hire the Kids: The Parental Guide

child receives everything they want materially without having to work for it. Parents or relatives may provide generous gifts, allowances, or other forms of financial support out of love. However, this can inadvertently create a sense of entitlement that makes the child feel they deserve things without earning them.

This entitlement mindset can lead to a host of problems, including a lack of motivation, a poor work ethic, and unrealistic expectations about life and work. When children are used to getting what they want without effort, they may struggle to adapt to situations where they have to earn their way, whether in school, work, or personal relationships.

In contrast, the Rich Kid model emphasizes empowerment through earning. By working for wages in a business owned solely by their parents, the Rich Kid learns the value of hard work and the satisfaction that comes from earning their own money. This experience fosters independence, self-sufficiency, and a strong work ethic, all of which are essential for success in adulthood.

Moreover, earning money through work helps the Rich Kid develop a healthy relationship with money. They understand that money is not just something that is given to them but something that is earned through effort and skill. This perspective can help them avoid the pitfalls of entitlement and develop a mindset that values hard work, responsibility, and financial discipline.

For example, a Rich Kid who is responsible for managing a specific aspect of the family business, such as inventory or customer service, will quickly learn that their performance has a direct impact on the business's success. This responsibility not only teaches them valuable skills but also reinforces the importance of earning and managing money wisely.

On the other hand, a Poor Kid who grows up with a sense of entitlement may struggle to find motivation in the workforce, where rewards are not guaranteed, and success requires effort and persistence. This entitlement mindset can lead to frustration, disappointment, and financial instability, as the child may lack the

Hire the Kids: The Parental Guide

resilience and work ethic needed to navigate the challenges of adulthood.

The Risks of Nepotism

Nepotism, or the practice of favoring relatives for employment or other opportunities, is another factor that can contribute to a Poor Kid mindset. While hiring a child in a family business can provide valuable experience, it can also lead to negative outcomes if not handled properly.

When nepotism is based on favoritism rather than merit, it can create a toxic work environment where the child is perceived as receiving special treatment without earning their position. This can lead to resentment among other employees, a lack of accountability for the child, and ultimately, harm the business's reputation and success.

The Rich Kid model, however, is based on meritocracy. In this model, the child's role in the business is earned through their skills, abilities, and contributions. The child is held accountable for their work, with accurate timecard records and skill-based job descriptions that are age-appropriate and aligned with the business's needs. This meritocratic approach ensures that the work produced by the Rich Kid benefits the operations of the company and preserves the family legacy.

By focusing on merit rather than kinship, the Rich Kid model helps the child develop a strong work ethic, a sense of responsibility, and a commitment to excellence. These qualities are essential for success in any field and can help the child build a reputation based on their abilities rather than their family connections.

In contrast, a Poor Kid who benefits from nepotism without being held accountable for their work may develop a sense of entitlement, laziness, or a lack of respect for the value of hard work. This can lead to long-term negative consequences, both for the child's personal development and for the business as a whole.

For example, suppose a child is given a high-level position in the family business without the necessary skills or experience. In that

Hire the Kids: The Parental Guide

case, they may struggle to perform effectively, leading to mistakes and inefficiencies and potentially harming the business's reputation. Moreover, this lack of accountability can prevent the child from developing the skills and work ethic needed to succeed independently, limiting their future opportunities.

In contrast, a Rich Kid who earns their position through merit and hard work is more likely to develop the skills, confidence, and resilience needed to succeed in any environment. This meritocratic approach not only benefits the child but also strengthens the family business, ensuring its long-term success and sustainability.

The Challenges of Side Hustles

In today's gig economy, many young people are turning to side hustles as a way to earn extra money. While side hustles can provide valuable experience and income, they also come with challenges that can contribute to a Poor Kid mindset.

One of the primary challenges of side hustles is the lack of stability and long-term benefits. Unlike traditional employment, where workers may receive benefits such as health insurance, retirement plans, and job security, side hustles often come with none of these perks. This lack of stability can make it difficult for young people to plan for the future, save for retirement, or build wealth.

Moreover, side hustles often require long hours and significant effort for relatively low pay. Many young people who take on side hustles quickly learn that they are not going to get rich from these ventures. After deductions for taxes, self-employment fees, and other expenses, the income from side hustles can be surprisingly low, leaving little room for savings or investment.

In contrast, the Rich Kid model emphasizes earning tax-free wages through a family business. By working for their parents, the Rich Kids can earn a stable income without the burden of taxes or other deductions, giving them a significant advantage when it comes to saving money and accumulating wealth.

Hire the Kids: The Parental Guide

For example, a Rich Kid who earns $12,000 a year working in a family business can save or invest that money entirely, whereas a peer who earns the same amount through a side hustle might only take home a fraction of that after taxes and expenses. This tax advantage allows the Rich Kid to accumulate wealth more quickly and efficiently, setting them up for long-term financial success.

Furthermore, working in a family business provides the Rich Kid with opportunities to develop skills and gain experience in a structured and supportive environment. Unlike side hustles, which can be isolating and lack mentorship, a family business offers the Rich Kid the chance to learn from experienced professionals, receive guidance and feedback, and build a strong foundation for future success.

In contrast, a Poor Kid who relies on side hustles may struggle to develop the skills and experience needed for long-term career growth. The lack of stability, mentorship, and benefits in side hustles can make it difficult for young people to achieve financial independence and build a secure future.

The Superior Financial Path of the Rich Kid

The Rich Kid vs. Everybody framework highlights the stark differences in financial education, opportunities, and outcomes between children who are strategically raised to understand the value of hard work, financial discipline, and entrepreneurship and those who are not. While the Poor Kid may face challenges related to inherited wealth, entitlement, nepotism, and side hustles, the Rich Kid benefits from a structured approach to earning, saving, and investing that sets them up for long-term success.

By earning tax-free wages through a family business, learning to budget and delay gratification, investing early in retirement accounts, and developing entrepreneurial skills, the Rich Kid is equipped with the tools and knowledge needed to achieve financial independence and build a prosperous future. In contrast, the Poor Kid may struggle with financial instability, a lack of motivation, and limited opportunities for growth.

Hire the Kids: The Parental Guide

For parents who own businesses, the Rich Kid model offers a powerful way to prepare their children for a successful future. By involving their children in the family business, teaching them financial literacy, and holding them accountable for their work, parents can instill the values and skills needed for long-term financial success. This approach not only benefits the child but also strengthens the family business, ensuring its legacy for generations to come.

Hire the Kids: The Parental Guide

CHAPTER 5: Building Wealth and Legacy

For many sole proprietors and small business owners, the goals driving their work go beyond immediate financial gain. They are building a legacy, aiming for sustained growth, leveraging tax deductions to optimize their finances, and working towards personal debt reduction. These outcomes are not just about creating a successful business; they are about securing a prosperous future for the next generation. The Rich Kid model—where children are integrated into the family business, earning tax-free wages, learning to manage finances through budgeting, starting early with investments, and developing entrepreneurial skills—serves as a comprehensive strategy to achieve these goals. By adopting this model, you can ensure that your children not only contribute meaningfully to the family business but also grow into financially savvy, responsible adults who are well-prepared to carry forward your business legacy.

Tax-Free Wages from Family Businesses

Integrating your child into your family business and maximizing the tax-free wages they can earn is not only a smart financial move but also a significant step towards achieving business tax deductions. When your child works for your sole proprietorship or family-owned business, the wages paid to them are deductible as a business expense, reducing the overall taxable income of the business. Moreover, if your child is under 18 and the business is not incorporated, their wages are exempt from Social Security and Medicare taxes, providing additional tax savings.

Tracking Hours Worked: One of the most effective ways to ensure your child is fairly compensated and that the business benefits from the tax deductions is by implementing a strict time-tracking system. This could involve using time-tracking software or a physical timecard where your child logs their working hours accurately. Not only does this practice instill discipline in your child, teaching them the importance of punctuality and accountability, but it also ensures that you have precise records needed for tax purposes. These records are essential during tax season to substantiate the wages paid and claim the appropriate deductions.

Understanding the Business: Encouraging your child to learn about various aspects of the business goes beyond just helping them understand what they are being paid to do. When children gain a holistic understanding of how the business operates—from supply chain management to customer relations—they are more likely to appreciate their role in the business and contribute more meaningfully. This involvement deepens their connection to the business and enhances their sense of responsibility, ultimately leading to more productive work that genuinely benefits the company.

Setting Work Goals: By helping your child set specific, measurable goals for their work, you not only give them a sense of purpose and achievement but also ensure that their contributions align with the business's strategic objectives. For instance, if your child is tasked with managing inventory, setting a goal to reduce waste by a certain percentage can have a direct positive impact on the business's bottom line. These work goals can also serve as a basis for evaluating their performance, making it easier to justify the wages paid and the associated tax deductions.

Participating in Business Meetings: Involving your child in business meetings or planning sessions exposes them to the decision-making processes that are critical to running a successful business. This exposure helps them understand the complexities of business management and the importance of strategic thinking. By participating in these meetings, your child can also contribute fresh ideas and perspectives, which can lead to innovative solutions and improvements in the business. This active participation not only prepares your child for future leadership roles but also helps the business grow, which in turn can lead to greater financial stability and the ability to take advantage of more tax deductions.

Hire the Kids: The Parental Guide

Delayed Gratification and Budgeting Skills

Personal growth, particularly in the areas of entrepreneurship and finance, is one of the most significant benefits of the Rich Kid model. Teaching your child to cultivate delayed gratification and master budgeting skills is foundational to their financial literacy and entrepreneurial mindset. These skills not only help them manage their finances effectively but also prepare them to make sound financial decisions in the future—whether in their own business ventures or in managing the family business.

Creating a Personal Budget: Encouraging your child to create a zero-based budget where every dollar they earn is allocated to a specific category—saving, spending, or investing—teaches them the importance of financial planning. This habit of thoughtful spending and saving is a critical aspect of personal growth. It helps children understand the value of money, prioritize their financial goals, and avoid impulsive spending. As they grow older, these budgeting skills will be invaluable in managing their finances and making informed financial decisions in business.

Setting Long-Term Savings Goals: Setting long-term financial goals is an excellent way to teach children about the benefits of delayed gratification. Whether they are saving for a significant purchase, college, or starting their own business, the process of setting and working towards these goals instills discipline and patience. This practice is particularly beneficial for their growth as future entrepreneurs, as it reinforces the importance of planning, perseverance, and the ability to think long-term—qualities that are essential for success in any business.

Tracking Expenses: Regularly tracking expenses and comparing them against their budget helps children identify areas where they can save more or cut unnecessary spending. This activity not only enhances their budgeting skills but also teaches them to be mindful of their spending habits. As they become more aware of where their money is going, they develop a stronger sense of financial responsibility, which is crucial for personal growth and success in both individual and business finances.

Hire the Kids: The Parental Guide

Using Financial Apps: Introducing children to budgeting apps like YNAB (You Need A Budget) or Mint makes the process of managing finances more engaging and easier to maintain. These tools help children visualize their budget, track their progress toward financial goals, and adjust their spending habits as needed. By integrating technology into their financial education, you are equipping them with the skills they need to navigate the increasingly digital world of finance. This tech-savvy approach to budgeting and financial management can also inspire them to explore and adopt new tools and strategies in their future business endeavors.

Early Investment in Retirement Accounts

Early investment in retirement accounts is a powerful strategy for long-term wealth accumulation, and it also plays a crucial role in helping your family reduce debt. By encouraging your child to start investing early, particularly in tax-advantaged accounts like a Roth IRA, you are setting the stage for significant financial growth over time. This early start not only helps them build wealth but also teaches them the importance of planning for the future and avoiding the pitfalls of debt.

Opening a Roth IRA: Helping your child open a Roth IRA is one of the most impactful steps you can take to secure their financial future. Contributions to a Roth IRA are made with after-tax dollars, meaning the money increases tax-free, and qualified withdrawals in retirement are also tax-free. Starting a Roth IRA at a young age allows your child to benefit from decades of compound interest, which can lead to substantial savings by the time they reach retirement age. This early investment strategy is particularly advantageous because it teaches your child the value of long-term planning and the power of compound interest, both of which are critical to avoiding debt and achieving financial independence.

Learning About Investment Options: Educating your child on different types of investments—stocks, bonds, mutual funds—and how they work helps them make informed decisions about where to invest their money. Understanding these basics not only empowers them to manage their Roth IRA effectively but also prepares them

Hire the Kids: The Parental Guide

to make smart investment choices in the future. This knowledge can prevent them from falling into common debt traps, such as taking on high-interest loans or credit card debt, by enabling them to grow their wealth through informed investments instead.

Setting Up Automatic Contributions: Teaching your child to automate their savings by setting up automatic contributions to their investment accounts ensures they consistently save without having to think about it. This habit of automatic saving is a powerful tool for debt reduction, as it prioritizes saving over spending and helps your child build a solid financial cushion. By consistently contributing to their Roth IRA, they can accumulate significant savings over time, reducing the likelihood that they will need to rely on debt to cover future expenses.

Monitoring and Reviewing Investments: Encouraging your child to regularly review their investment portfolio and understand how their investments are performing teaches them to be proactive in managing their finances. This practice not only helps individuals learn about market trends and develop a long-term investment strategy but also reinforces the importance of staying informed and making necessary adjustments. By developing these habits early, your child is more likely to avoid costly financial mistakes that could lead to debt and financial insecurity.

Developing Entrepreneurial Skills Through Work

One of the most significant outcomes of the Rich Kid model is the legacy it creates within the family business. By developing entrepreneurial skills through meaningful work experience, children not only contribute to the success of the business but also prepare themselves to carry on the family legacy. This approach ensures that the business remains strong and prosperous for future generations while also instilling in children the values and skills needed to succeed as entrepreneurs.

Starting a Small Business Venture: Encouraging your child to start a small business, such as a lemonade stand, lawn mowing service, or online shop, is an excellent way to teach them the basics of entrepreneurship and business management. This hands-on experience gives them the opportunity to apply the skills they've learned in the family business to their own venture, fostering creativity, problem-solving, and independence. By starting their own business, they also gain a deeper understanding of the challenges and rewards of entrepreneurship, which is essential for carrying on the family legacy.

Involving Them in Marketing: Allowing your child to take part in marketing efforts for the family business, such as managing social media accounts or creating promotional materials, helps them understand the importance of customer engagement and branding. This experience not only teaches them valuable marketing skills but also gives them a sense of ownership and responsibility for the business's success. By involving them in marketing, you are preparing them to take on leadership roles in the future and ensuring that the business remains relevant and competitive in the marketplace.

Solving Business Problems: Challenging your child to identify a problem within the business and develop a solution encourages critical thinking and innovation. Whether it's improving customer service, streamlining operations, or creating a new product, these problem-solving experiences help your child develop the skills and confidence needed to overcome challenges and drive the business forward. This ability to innovate and adapt is crucial for maintaining the business's success and ensuring its long-term viability.

Attending Entrepreneurial Workshops: Enrolling your child in workshops or courses focused on entrepreneurship provides valuable knowledge and networking opportunities that will help them in their entrepreneurial journey. These programs offer insights into the latest trends and strategies in business, as well as the opportunity to learn from successful entrepreneurs. By participating in these workshops, your child gains a broader perspective on entrepreneurship and develops the skills and connections needed to continue the family legacy and build a successful business of their own.

The Rich Kid Model as a Pathway to Success

Hire the Kids: The Parental Guide

The Rich Kid model is not just about providing children with financial education and work experience; it is a comprehensive strategy for achieving the key outcomes that many sole proprietors and small business owners strive for: legacy, growth, tax benefits, and debt reduction. By integrating children into the family business, teaching them to manage their finances, encouraging early investment, and fostering entrepreneurial skills, parents can ensure that their children are well-prepared for the challenges and opportunities of the future.

This model helps children develop a strong foundation in financial literacy, work ethic, and entrepreneurship, setting the stage for a prosperous future. At the same time, it supports the family's business goals by leveraging tax deductions, promoting business growth, reducing personal debt, and ensuring the continuation of the family legacy.

Hire the Kids: The Parental Guide

Hire the Kids: The Parental Guide

CHAPTER 6: A Parent's Guide to the "Rich Kid" Model

This book aims to bridge the gap by offering parents step-by-step instructions on how to involve their children in the family business. It's about transitioning from a model where children might passively receive an allowance without understanding its value to one where they earn income through meaningful work, learn to manage their finances, appreciate the power of investment, and develop valuable skills and entrepreneurial insights.

Section 1: Child Labor Laws and Regulations

Child labor laws are designed to ensure the safety and well-being of young workers across the country, safeguarding them from exploitation and hazardous working conditions. These regulations are critical for maintaining a standard of safety and fairness in the workplace. However, the federal government also acknowledges the unique and beneficial circumstances under which children can work for their parents' small businesses. This recognition allows for certain exceptions within the child labor laws, permitting children to gain invaluable work experience and financial knowledge under the supervision of their parents.

The regulations surrounding child labor vary significantly from state to state, reflecting the diverse values, economic conditions, and legislative priorities of each region. While federal laws provide a broad framework, state-specific regulations often add layers of complexity, making it essential for parents to understand both federal and state requirements.

To navigate these regulations effectively, start by visiting the U.S. Department of Labor's official website. Here, you can access comprehensive information on federal child labor laws, including permissible working hours, age restrictions, and the types of work that are considered safe and appropriate for minors. This federal

Hire the Kids: The Parental Guide

overview serves as a foundation for understanding the basic legal landscape.

Next, delve into the specifics of your state's labor laws by locating the portal for your state's labor department or equivalent agency. Conducting a simple search query like "[Your State] child labor laws" can direct you to the relevant resources. State regulations may have additional requirements or more stringent restrictions compared to federal laws. For instance, while federal law may allow children to work in their family's business at any age, some states might impose minimum age requirements or limit the number of hours minors can work, especially during school days.

Reviewing age restrictions and permitted work categories is crucial. Pay special attention to provisions specific to family-owned businesses. These rules often distinguish between general employment and family business employment, recognizing the controlled and supportive environment that a family business can offer. For example, tasks that involve heavy machinery or hazardous materials are typically off-limits, but many administrative or customer service roles are permissible.

Consider the case of the Johnson family in Texas, who own a small bakery. By understanding and complying with both federal and Texas state labor laws, they successfully involved their 14-year-old son in their business. He began by managing social media accounts and assisting with inventory, tasks that were both age-appropriate and legally permissible. This practical involvement provided him with a robust understanding of business operations while staying within legal boundaries.

If there is any uncertainty or if the regulations appear complex, it is advisable to contact local authorities for clarification. Reaching out to your state labor department via email or phone can provide precise information and resolve any ambiguities regarding permissible work, hours, and conditions. Experts recommend keeping a detailed record of all communications and confirmations from these authorities to ensure you have proof of compliance if needed.

Hire the Kids: The Parental Guide

Understanding and complying with child labor laws is not only a legal obligation but also a fundamental step in creating a safe and educational work environment for your child. By ensuring that the work is age-appropriate and legally sanctioned, you foster a setting where your child can learn valuable skills and gain work experience without compromising their safety or well-being.

Safety and Well-being

When minors work in a business owned by their parents, it is crucial to understand what constitutes a hazardous work environment. Even though children working for their parents in a family-owned business often benefit from more lenient regulations compared to other types of employment, federal and state laws still set strict guidelines to ensure the safety and well-being of your child. A hazardous work environment for a minor presents risks or dangers that could cause harm, injury, or illness.

Dangerous machinery and equipment are common hazards in many workplaces. For minors, exposure to machinery with moving parts, such as power-driven hoisting apparatuses, meat slicers, meat processing machines, circular saws, band saws, and woodchippers, poses significant risks of cutting, crushing, or trapping body parts. Heavy machinery, including forklifts, tractors, and cranes, also presents serious dangers due to the potential for severe injury if the equipment is mishandled.

Work environments involving hazardous substances or chemicals create additional risks for minors. Toxic chemicals, often found in industrial cleaning, automotive repair, or certain manufacturing processes, can cause respiratory issues, skin irritation, burns, or even long-term health problems. Minors also face significant dangers when working near flammable or explosive materials, such as those found in welding shops or gas stations, due to the high risk of fire or explosions.

Construction and demolition sites present another set of hazards for young workers. Jobs requiring work at heights, such as on ladders, scaffolding, or roofs, are particularly dangerous, as falls can result in serious injuries or fatalities. These sites often have loose debris, unstable structures, or falling objects, all of which pose significant risks to minors.

Extreme temperatures and high noise levels can also create hazardous environments for minors. Working in environments with excessive heat or cold, such as commercial kitchens, foundries, or freezers, can lead to burns, heatstroke, hypothermia, or frostbite. High noise levels, common in some manufacturing facilities, can result in hearing damage, with minors being especially vulnerable to noise-induced hearing loss.

Assignments that involve heavy lifting or physically demanding tasks can also be hazardous for minors. Repeatedly lifting heavy objects or engaging in strenuous physical labor can lead to musculoskeletal injuries, as young bodies are more susceptible to strain and injury. Overexertion from intense manual work, such as moving heavy boxes, can also cause injuries.

Additionally, exposure to biological hazards poses significant risks to minors. Environments where they could encounter bloodborne pathogens, viruses, or bacteria, such as hospitals, veterinary clinics, or biological research labs, are considered unsafe.

The Fair Labor Standards Act (FLSA) outlines the types of work minors can perform and the environments in which they can work to protect young workers from hazardous conditions. Children under the age of 14 generally cannot work in non-agricultural jobs except in specific cases, such as acting or delivering newspapers. Minors aged 14-15 can work in non-hazardous environments and are limited to jobs considered safe, such as office work or cashiering. Although minors aged 16-17 can work in a broader range of environments, they are still prohibited from jobs classified as hazardous by the Department of Labor, including those involving dangerous machinery, chemicals, or heights.

Parents who own businesses must assess the work environment carefully and identify any potential hazards that could pose risks to their children. Even in family-owned businesses, following these

Hire the Kids: The Parental Guide

regulations is essential to ensure the safety of young workers. Regularly review the minor's work environment to identify any dangers and implement measures to mitigate risks. Install safety guards on machinery, provide appropriate personal protective equipment (PPE), and ensure proper ventilation in areas where chemicals are used. Provide thorough training to minors on safety protocols and proper equipment usage, and maintain continuous supervision, especially for younger workers, to ensure they follow safety procedures. Business owners should also familiarize themselves with the child labor laws specific to their state, as these laws can vary and may include additional requirements beyond federal regulations.

Parents must prioritize their children's safety and education while introducing them to the world of work. Properly navigating child labor laws ensures that your children benefit from working in the family business and gain practical skills and financial literacy within a secure and supportive environment. This balance between legal compliance and educational enrichment is essential for leveraging the advantages of early work experiences in family-owned businesses.

While child labor laws can appear restrictive, they are designed to protect young workers. By understanding and working within these laws, parents can provide their children with meaningful and educational work experiences that will benefit them in the long term. The unique circumstances of family-owned businesses offer a valuable opportunity to teach children about work, responsibility, and financial literacy in a safe and supportive setting.

1. **Start with the Department of Labor Website:** Visit the U.S. Department of Labor's official website and navigate to the "Child Labor" section for a federal overview.

2. **Seek State-Specific Information:** Locate the portal for your state's labor department or equivalent agency. This is often

Hire the Kids: The Parental Guide

found via a simple search engine query such as "<Your State> child labor laws."

3. **Review Age Restrictions and Permitted Work:** Look for information specific to family-owned businesses, focusing on age restrictions, allowed hours, and types of permissible work.
4. **Contact Local Authorities:** If in doubt, reach out to your state labor department directly via email or phone for clarification.

Hire the Kids: The Parental Guide

Section 2: Compensation and Accountability

Paying your child for genuine work within your family business not only instills a strong sense of responsibility but also brings significant financial and tax benefits. However, this process must be approached with careful planning, diligence, and adherence to legal standards to ensure that the arrangement is beneficial and compliant with regulations.

First and foremost, employing your child in your business helps them develop a robust work ethic. When children earn money through actual work, they learn the value of labor and the effort required to make money. This experience is vastly different from receiving an allowance, which may not always correlate with the effort expended. By working in the family business, children understand the direct relationship between work and financial reward, which is a fundamental lesson in financial literacy. For example, the Johnson family, who runs a local bakery, involved their 15-year-old daughter in managing social media and customer service. This not only improved her communication skills but also taught her about marketing and customer engagement.

In addition to fostering responsibility, paying your child can offer substantial financial benefits. When children earn their own money, they gain practical financial management skills. They learn to budget, save, and even invest their earnings, setting the foundation for sound financial habits. Opening a custodial bank account for your child's earnings is an excellent way to introduce them to banking. This account allows them to deposit their wages, manage their money, and understand the basics of banking transactions. Over time, these experiences can help them develop a healthy relationship with money and improve their financial literacy.

From a tax perspective, employing your child can be advantageous for both the family and the business. The wages paid to your child are deductible as a business expense, reducing the overall taxable income of the company. It is important to note that this deduction can result in significant tax savings, which is especially helpful for small businesses where every dollar counts. Additionally, it's

Hire the Kids: The Parental Guide

important to highlight that kids under 18 who work for a parent's sole-proprietorship or a partnership where both parents are the "only partners" are exempt from Medicare taxes and Social Security, providing further financial relief. This exemption further enhances the monetary benefit of employing your child. Financial advisors agree that this tax benefit can provide a substantial advantage for small businesses, making it a smart financial move to use your children.

However, to maximize these benefits, make sure the employment is legitimate and compliant with all relevant laws and regulations. Begin with creating a detailed job description that outlines your child's responsibilities, hours, and wages. The job description should match your child's abilities and be appropriate for their age. For instance, younger children might take on simpler tasks like filing documents or cleaning. In comparison, older children could handle more complex roles, such as managing social media accounts or assisting with bookkeeping.

Once the job description is established, set up a formal payroll system to pay your child. This system should accurately track hours worked and wages paid, ensuring that payments are made regularly and documented correctly. Proper documentation is essential not only for tax purposes but also to demonstrate that the employment arrangement is legitimate and that the wages are reasonable for the work performed.

It is also important to comply with child labor laws, which vary by state. These laws regulate the types of work children can perform, the hours they can work, and the conditions under which they work. Become familiar with both federal and state labor laws to ensure full compliance. For example, while federal law allows children of any age to work in a business owned by their parents, state laws might have additional restrictions, such as limiting work hours during the school year.

Opening a custodial account at a bank involves a straightforward process: visit your bank with your child, provide necessary documentation (such as your ID, your child's birth certificate, and

Hire the Kids: The Parental Guide

their Social Security number), and complete the application form. This account will serve as a practical tool for teaching your child how to manage their earnings responsibly.

Transferring funds to this account should be done transparently. Write checks or set up electronic transfers from your business account to your child's custodial account, clearly stating in the transaction memo that these are wages. This clarity is crucial for both accounting and educational purposes, helping your child understand the flow of money and the importance of record-keeping.

Another key aspect is ensuring that your child's wages are reasonable. Research the average wages for similar roles in your area and adjust the compensation based on your child's experience, age, and the complexity of the job. This approach not only complies with legal standards but also teaches your child about fair compensation and market value for work performed.

Tracking your child's working hours accurately is vital. Implement a timecard system or use time-tracking software to ensure that your child clocks in and out, recording their working hours precisely. This practice is not only essential for payroll processing but also instills in your child the discipline of time management and accountability.

It is important to think about the future possibilities that these experiences can offer. Children who acquire practical work experience in a family business often discover that these skills are greatly appreciated in higher education and professional environments. Colleges and employers look favorably upon applicants who have demonstrated responsibility, initiative, and a strong work ethic from a young age. Additionally, the entrepreneurial skills they develop can inspire them to start their businesses or pursue innovative projects.

However, integrating children into the family business is not without challenges. Balancing work and education can be difficult, and it's essential to ensure that your child's academic responsibilities are addressed. Open communication and setting clear boundaries between work and school can help manage this balance effectively.

Hire the Kids: The Parental Guide

In summary, paying your child for genuine work within your family business offers multiple benefits, including fostering a sense of responsibility, enhancing financial literacy, and providing tax advantages. To fully realize these advantages, the process must be approached with meticulous planning and strict compliance with all relevant laws and regulations. By creating detailed job descriptions, setting up a formal payroll system, ensuring reasonable wages, and maintaining accurate records, you can create a professional and educational work environment for your child that prepares them for future financial independence and success. Incorporating expert advice and real-world examples and acknowledging potential challenges and solutions makes this process more practical and beneficial for the entire family.

Job Descriptions and Accountability

Create Detailed Job Descriptions: Outline clear responsibilities that match your child's abilities. This legitimizes their employment and sets expectations.

Documenting Work Over $600 Annually

Be aware that compensating your child over $600 in a year requires filing a W-2 form. The threshold for minimum deductible contributions will also be relevant here.

1. **Opening a Custodial Checking Account:**
    1. Visit your bank with your child.
    2. Provide necessary documentation (your ID, your child's birth certificate, and Social Security number).
    3. Complete the application form for a custodial account.

2. **Transferring Funds:**
    1. Write a check or set up an electronic transfer from your business account to your child's custodial account.

2. Ensure the transaction memo/details clearly state it's for wages.

3. **Ensuring Reasonable Wages:**
    1. Research average wages for similar roles and responsibilities.
    2. Adjust compensation based on your child's experience, age, and job complexity.

4. **Tracking Time:**
    1. Implement a timecard system or subscribe to time-tracking software.
    2. Ensure your child clocks in and out to record their working hours accurately.

Hire the Kids: The Parental Guide

Hire the Kids: The Parental Guide

Section 3: Taxation and Documentation

The taxation landscape for employing your child is designed to provide significant benefits for family-owned businesses while ensuring compliance and fairness in the tax system. By understanding and navigating these tax laws, you can not only save money but also instill valuable financial and work ethics in your children.

Deducting your kid's wages as a business expense is one of the most significant advantages of employing your child in a family-owned business. It creates the possibility for substantial tax savings. When you reduce your business's overall taxable income, this potentially lowers the amount of taxes owed. For many small businesses, this can result in significant financial benefits. To qualify for this deduction, the wages paid to your child must be reasonable and commensurate with the work they perform. The IRS requires that compensation be fair market value for the services rendered, so it's crucial to document the job description, hours worked, and wages paid.

Consider the example of the Martinez family, who run a successful landscaping business. By employing their teenage son to assist with bookkeeping and customer scheduling, they not only provided him with valuable work experience but also saved thousands of dollars in business expenses. Keeping detailed records and maintaining a formal payroll system helped substantiate these expenses during tax time and ensured compliance with IRS regulations.

Additionally, if your child's total income remains below the standard deduction threshold, they may not owe any federal income taxes. This means that if your child earns less than the standard deduction amount, they would not be required to pay federal income taxes on their earnings. This can be a strategic way to shift income within the family, reducing the overall tax burden while providing your child with valuable work experience and income.

Employing your child also opens the door to other tax-advantaged financial planning opportunities. For instance, you can help your child contribute to a Roth IRA. Even though they are minors, if they

Hire the Kids: The Parental Guide

have earned income, they are eligible to contribute to an IRA. When you contribute to a Roth IRA, you are utilizing after-tax dollars, and the earnings grow tax-free. In retirement, qualified withdrawals are also tax-free. Starting a Roth IRA at a young age allows your child to take advantage of decades of compound growth, setting them up for a financially secure future. Financial advisors emphasize early contributions to a Roth IRA can significantly impact a child's economic future, providing them with a substantial nest egg by the time they retire."

Why the Government Allows Children to Work for Parents Without Payroll Taxes

In the United States, children working for their parents' businesses, particularly in sole proprietorships or family partnerships, enjoy certain exemptions from standard payroll taxes, such as Social Security and Medicare. This exemption reflects a unique intersection of family dynamics, economic encouragement, and tax policy aimed at supporting family-run enterprises. Understanding why the government provides these exemptions requires examining the legal framework and the underlying social and economic rationale.

Under the Fair Labor Standards Act (FLSA) and the Internal Revenue Code, children employed by their parents in a family-owned business are exempt from specific payroll taxes, including Social Security and Medicare taxes. This exemption typically applies if the child is under 18 and the business is a sole proprietorship or a partnership owned solely by the parents. The reasoning behind this exemption is multifaceted and rooted in several practical and economic considerations.

One of the primary reasons the government allows these exemptions is to encourage family-owned businesses. Small businesses form the backbone of the American economy, and family-run enterprises represent a significant portion of this sector. By allowing parents to employ their children without the additional financial burden of payroll taxes, the government is effectively supporting the growth and sustainability of small businesses. This policy helps family businesses reduce their operational costs while providing valuable

Hire the Kids: The Parental Guide

work experience for their children. By removing payroll tax obligations, the government incentivizes parents to involve their children in their businesses, promoting both economic education and family cohesion.

Another reason for this exemption is to minimize the administrative burden on small businesses. Calculating and withholding Social Security and Medicare taxes for a child employed by their parents can be cumbersome, especially for smaller operations that may not have the resources to handle complex payroll processing. By exempting these wages from payroll taxes, the government simplifies tax compliance for family-run businesses, permitting them to redirect more focus on their core operations and growth.

Regarding the question of whether this exemption exists because children are already covered under their parent's health insurance, reducing the likelihood of lawsuits, the connection is less direct. While it is true that minors are generally covered under their parent's health insurance plans, the primary motivation for the payroll tax exemption does not revolve around liability concerns or the potential for lawsuits.

In most family businesses, the relationship between parents and children involves a high degree of trust and shared responsibility. Parents are naturally motivated to ensure the safety and well-being of their children, reducing the likelihood of workplace injuries and subsequent legal action. Additionally, most family businesses would address any injury or accident internally, further minimizing the risk of litigation.

While the exemption from Social Security and Medicare taxes is not directly tied to insurance coverage or liability concerns, these factors indirectly support the rationale. Because parents typically provide health insurance coverage for their children, the government may perceive less need for the safety nets these payroll taxes provide, such as Social Security Disability Insurance and Medicare. The trust inherent in the parent-child relationship further supports the notion that family businesses are more likely to protect and care for their

Hire the Kids: The Parental Guide

young workers, lessening the need for the standard protections afforded by payroll taxes.

The exemption from Social Security and Medicare taxes for children working in family-owned businesses is a carefully considered policy that balances various social, economic, and practical considerations. By allowing parents to employ their children without the additional burden of payroll taxes, the government supports the growth of family businesses, encourages financial responsibility among young people, and simplifies tax compliance for small enterprises. While this exemption is not directly tied to health insurance coverage or liability concerns, these factors contribute to a broader understanding of why the policy exists.

Follow the proper strategies and maintain thorough documentation to maximize these benefits and ensure compliance. Here are some key steps to consider:

Create a Formal Job Description: Clearly outline your child's duties, responsibilities, and the skills required for the job. This document should detail the nature of the work and the expected hours. A formal job description helps justify the wages paid and ensures that the employment is legitimate.

Set Up a Payroll System: Even if your business is small, it's important to process payroll formally. Use payroll software or services that can handle tax withholdings, generate pay stubs, and provide year-end tax forms like W-2s. This system will ensure that all wages are documented properly and comply with tax regulations. QuickBooks is a popular option that can streamline this process.

Document Work Hours: Keep authentic records of your child's hours worked. This can be done using a timecard system, time-tracking software, or a simple logbook. Accurate records are crucial for substantiating the wages paid and for complying with labor laws.

Ensure Reasonable Wages: Pay your child a fair wage that aligns with the work they are performing. Research the typical salaries for similar jobs in your area to determine a reasonable rate. Overpaying

Hire the Kids: The Parental Guide

can raise red flags with the IRS and potentially disqualify the wages from being deductible.

Use Proper Tax Forms: Ensure all necessary tax forms are completed accurately. Your child will need to complete Form W-4 at the start of employment to determine withholding amounts. At the end of the year, a Form W-2 is issued to report their annual wages and taxes withheld. Additionally, you'll need to file these forms with the IRS.

Please consult with a Tax Professional: Given the complexities of tax regulations, it's wise to consult with a CPA or tax advisor. They can provide guidance specific to your situation, help ensure compliance, and identify additional tax-saving opportunities. Have a professional review of your setup; this can prevent costly mistakes and ensure you're taking full advantage of the available tax benefits."

In summary, the taxation landscape for employing your child in a family-owned business offers numerous benefits, including tax deductions, payroll tax exemptions, and valuable financial planning opportunities. By following best practices, consulting with professionals, and maintaining thorough documentation, you can create a beneficial and educational work environment for your child, positioning them for a course of financial literacy and responsibility while optimizing your business's tax situation.

Why the IRS Requires Paperwork

The Internal Revenue Service plays a vital role in regulating tax compliance for all types of employment in the United States, including when children work for their parents' businesses. While the IRS offers specific tax exemptions to children under 18 who work in their parents' sole proprietorship or partnership-owned businesses, these exemptions come with a set of strict paperwork requirements. These requirements aim to prevent tax evasion and ensure that children are genuinely employed and fairly compensated for their work.

The IRS mandates businesses to provide documentation to validate employment relationships, even when it involves family members.

Hire the Kids: The Parental Guide

This requirement is especially relevant for children under 18 who work in their parents' businesses, as these situations often appear more informal and could be prone to misuse. By requiring specific forms such as the W-4, W-2, and I-9, the IRS ensures transparency and accountability. The W-4 form helps the employer determine the amount of federal income tax to withhold from the employee's paycheck, while the W-2 form reports the wages paid to the employee and the taxes withheld throughout the year. The I-9 form verifies the identity and employment authorization of the employee. These forms play a critical role in ensuring that the employment is legitimate, that fair wages are paid, and that proper tax procedures are followed.

One of the main reasons the IRS requires meticulous paperwork for children employed in family businesses is to prevent tax evasion and fraud. Family businesses might face temptations to misclassify wages, report inflated deductions, or underreport income to reduce their tax liability. By demanding detailed documentation of employment, the IRS ensures that businesses accurately report all income and claim legitimate tax benefits. For example, when a parent employs their child and claims a wage expense on their tax return, the IRS needs assurance that the child performs actual work and receives reasonable compensation. Without proper documentation, businesses could easily manipulate payroll records, create fictitious jobs, or inflate wages to reduce taxable income. Such tax evasion not only deprives the government of revenue but also undermines the integrity of the tax system.

The IRS also has specific guidelines on what constitutes fair compensation for family members working in a business. The wages paid must reflect the market rate for the type of work performed. If a business owner pays their child an exorbitant salary for simple tasks, the IRS could view it as an attempt to shift income and reduce the parent's taxable income. By requiring paperwork that outlines job responsibilities, hours worked, and wages paid, the IRS can verify that compensation is fair and appropriate for the work performed.

Hire the Kids: The Parental Guide

Beyond preventing tax evasion, the IRS paperwork requirements ensure that children working in family businesses receive fair compensation and that their employment meets standard labor practices. These protections are crucial, as children working for their parents might be more vulnerable to exploitation or may not fully understand their rights as employees.

The exemption from Social Security and Medicare taxes for children under 18 working in their parents' businesses is designed to support family businesses and provide young people with valuable work experience. However, the IRS requires proof that these exemptions are applied correctly. The exemption applies only if the business is a sole proprietorship or a partnership owned solely by the parents and if the child genuinely works in the business. The employment must involve actual work and not just serve as a mechanism for the parents to reduce their tax liability. By mandating that businesses maintain accurate and detailed records of their employment practices, the IRS ensures that children receive fair payment and gain appropriate work experience and training. This requirement protects the child's long-term interests by helping them acquire valuable skills and work habits that will benefit them in the future.

Documentation serves as a critical tool for promoting transparency in the employment of children within family businesses. It provides a clear record of the employment relationship, including the duties assigned to the child, the hours worked, and the wages paid. This transparency helps protect both the business and the child, ensuring that all parties understand their rights and responsibilities. Maintaining proper records helps prevent disputes or misunderstandings regarding the terms of employment. If questions arise about the work performed or the compensation received, having detailed records allows both the business owner and the child to refer back to the original agreement. This clarity can help resolve potential conflicts and ensure a positive working relationship.

Furthermore, the IRS's requirement for documentation also protects businesses from allegations of unfair labor practices. By keeping accurate records of employment practices, businesses can demonstrate compliance with labor laws and IRS regulations, thereby safeguarding their reputation and avoiding potential legal issues.

Requiring paperwork for children employed in family businesses encourages responsible business practices that benefit both the employer and the employee. These practices include adhering to fair labor standards, maintaining accurate financial records, and ensuring that all employment is legitimate and properly documented.

Promoting responsible business practices through IRS requirements also protects the interests of the child. These practices ensure that children are not being exploited or used as a means to reduce the business's tax liability but are instead gaining meaningful work experience and being compensated fairly for their efforts.

The IRS's paperwork requirements for children working in family businesses protect the integrity of the tax system and reflect a careful balance between supporting family enterprises and ensuring compliance with tax laws. By requiring documentation, the IRS helps prevent tax evasion, ensures fair compensation, promotes transparency, and encourages responsible business practices.

Standard Paperwork for IRS Audit

1. **Form W-4**: Completed by your child at the start of employment for withholding purposes.

2. **Form W-2:** Issued to your child at the end of the year, reporting annual wages and taxes withheld.

3. **Form I-9:** Documentation verifying your child's eligibility to work in the U.S. legally.

Completing and Filing Paperwork

1. **Gather Information:** Collect all necessary personal and financial information from your child.

Hire the Kids: The Parental Guide

2. **Use IRS or Payroll Software:** Access the IRS website for tax form completion instructions or utilize payroll software to fill out forms accurately.

3. **Securely Store Documents**: Maintain physical on-premises files or digital copies of all forms and employment records or cloud storage for easy access and security.

Filing Paperwork Electronically

1. **Electronic Filing Options**: Investigate IRS e-file options or third-party software that supports electronic submission of tax documents.

2. **Backup Your Files:** Ensure all documents are backed up in multiple storage locations.

3. **Stay Informed on Deadlines:** Keep track of submission deadlines for each form to avoid penalties.

Section 4: Bookkeepers and Tracking Labor Costs

Accurate bookkeeping forms the foundation of any thriving small business. With it, companies may avoid financial challenges, penalties, and missed opportunities. A bookkeeper's role is vital in upholding financial clarity and compliance. Their expertise ensures precise tracking of every dollar spent or earned, which is especially important for labor expenses, whether involving your child or external labor. Employing a bookkeeper offers invaluable support, allowing you to focus on business growth while maintaining meticulous and compliant financial records.

Bookkeepers possess vast knowledge and expertise. They have a deep understanding of accounting software, tax laws, and financial reporting, making them invaluable for small business owners. By meticulously tracking income and expenses, a bookkeeper can help you make well-informed business decisions, proactively identify potential financial issues, and optimize your tax deductions.

Modern bookkeeping leverages advanced technology and software to streamline processes. Tools like QuickBooks, Xero, and FreshBooks have revolutionized how small businesses manage their finances. These platforms deliver features such as automated invoicing, real-time financial tracking, and seamless integration with bank accounts, making it easier than ever to keep accurate records.

Choosing the Right Bookkeeper: Look for a certified professional with experience in your industry and a solid track record. Ask for references.

Clear Communication: Establish clear lines of communication. Schedule recurring meetings to discuss business goals and review financial reports.

Transparency: Provide your bookkeeper with all necessary information and access to financial documents. Transparency is key to accurate bookkeeping and financial planning.

One common challenge small businesses face is managing cash flow. A bookkeeper can help by providing detailed cash flow statements and projections, allowing you to anticipate shortfalls and make informed decisions to keep your business solvent.

Bookkeepers stay updated on the latest regulations and tax laws. But you should be aware the future of bookkeeping is set to be shaped by several emerging trends:

Automation and AI: Automation tools and AI are becoming increasingly prevalent, handling repetitive tasks and reducing the risk of human error.

Cloud-Based Solutions: Cloud technology allows for real-time data access and collaboration from anywhere, making it easier to manage finances on the go.

Hire the Kids: The Parental Guide

Data Analytics: Advanced data analytics provide deeper insights into financial performance, helping businesses to optimize operations and increase profitability.

Blockchain Technology: Blockchain promises enhanced security and transparency in financial transactions, potentially revolutionizing bookkeeping practices.

In conclusion, the role of a bookkeeper in a small business cannot be overstated. Their expertise in managing payroll, tracking labor expenses, maintaining the general ledger, and ensuring tax compliance is essential for financial clarity and compliance. By providing accurate financial records and strategic insights, bookkeepers enable small business owners to make informed decisions, optimize their operations, and focus on growing their businesses. Whether you are employing family members or outside labor, a bookkeeper's meticulous attention to detail and comprehensive understanding of financial management can significantly benefit your business.

Importance of Working with a Bookkeeper

A bookkeeper helps you manage your business's financial records, ensuring accuracy and compliance with tax laws. They are instrumental in tracking labor expenses, which can be complex due to varying rates, hours, and tax implications. By maintaining precise records, a bookkeeper can help you make informed business decisions, budget effectively, and prepare for tax time without surprises.

Tracking the labor expenses of your children who work for your sole proprietorship business serves several essential purposes, encompassing financial, legal, and educational aspects. Meticulous tracking is essential for accurately documenting all financial transactions, ensuring the integrity of your business's financial records. This transparency not only aids in precise accounting and budgeting but also reinforces the professional nature of the employment relationship, emphasizing to your children the significance of accountability and financial discipline.

Hire the Kids: The Parental Guide

One of the most significant advantages of tracking these expenses is the immediate financial benefit. By deducting wages paid to your children as a legitimate business expense, you can substantially reduce your business's taxable income. For example, if you pay your child a reasonable wage for their work, this expense can be deducted from your business income, thereby lowering your overall tax liability. However, it's important to create and maintain detailed records of hours worked, wages paid, and job descriptions to substantiate these deductions. Without proper documentation, you risk disallowance of these deductions during an audit, which could lead to penalties and increased tax liabilities.

In addition, it is important to accurately track labor expenses to ensure compliance with both federal and state labor laws. These regulations outline specific requirements concerning the employment of minors, including permissible work hours, types of tasks, and wage standards. By maintaining detailed records, you can demonstrate adherence to these laws, thereby avoiding potential legal issues and penalties. For example, federal laws allow children of any age to work in a business owned by their parents, but state laws might impose additional restrictions. Ensuring that your child's work hours and job responsibilities are well-documented and compliant with these regulations is critical.

Tracking labor expenses is not just about financial and legal aspects but also about fostering a sense of financial responsibility and work ethic in your children. When children see their efforts being acknowledged and their earnings documented, it helps them understand the value of their work. This process teaches them important life skills, such as time management, the value of labor, and the principles of financial management. By issuing paychecks and maintaining formal employment records, you provide your children with real-world experience that prepares them for future employment opportunities, both within and outside the family business.

Apart from offering educational benefits for your children, precise tracking of labor expenses can significantly enhance overall business management. It enables you to analyze labor costs accurately,

Hire the Kids: The Parental Guide

pinpointing areas for improvement and potential cost reductions. For instance, by reviewing the time and tasks your children undertake, you might find opportunities to streamline operations or reallocate resources more effectively. This level of insight is particularly valuable for small businesses, where labor costs can significantly impact profitability.

Furthermore, tracking labor expenses contributes to better financial planning and forecasting. With accurate records, you can project future labor costs more reliably, which aids in budgeting and financial strategy development. This foresight helps ensure that your business remains financially healthy and can adapt to changing economic conditions or business demands. For example, if you plan to expand your business or introduce new products or services, understanding your labor expenses can help you make informed decisions about staffing and resource allocation.

Moreover, involving your children in the process of tracking their work hours and understanding their wages can further enhance their learning experience. Encourage them to use time-tracking apps or logbooks to record their hours and tasks. Reviewing these records together can provide valuable teaching moments about accountability, honesty, and the importance of detailed record-keeping in business operations. This practice not only benefits your business but also equips your children with practical skills that will serve them well in any career.

Ensuring the accurate tracking of labor expenses is crucial in order to avoid potential legal repercussions. In the absence of thorough documentation, there is a risk of facing penalties for non-compliance with labor laws. In the event of an audit, the possibility of being required to pay back taxes, as well as fines, exists. Accurate record-keeping protects your business from these risks and ensures that you are fully compliant with all regulations.

In conclusion, tracking the labor expenses of your children who work for your sole proprietorship is a multifaceted practice that brings numerous benefits. It ensures financial accuracy, maximizes tax benefits, and maintains compliance with labor laws. Additionally,

Hire the Kids: The Parental Guide

it fosters financial responsibility and work ethic in your children, enhances business management, and aids in financial planning and forecasting. By leveraging modern accounting tools and involving your children in the tracking process, you can create a professional and educational work environment that prepares them for future success while optimizing your business operations. This comprehensive approach to managing labor expenses underscores the value of meticulous financial tracking and its impact on both personal and business growth.

Tracking Labor Expenses in QuickBooks

1. **Set Up Employees or Contractors:** In QuickBooks, start by setting up a profile for each individual working for you, categorizing them correctly as employees or contractors.

2. **Enter Time Worked:** Use the Time Tracking feature to record the hours worked by each person. This can be entered manually or through integrated time-tracking apps.

3. **Run Payroll:** For employees, use QuickBooks Payroll to process payments. This automatically updates your labor expenses.

4. **Record Payments to Contractors:** For outside labor classified as contractors, record payments using the "Expenses" or "Cheques" feature, depending on how you compensate them.

Coding Your General Ledger (GL) for Labor Expenses

Labor Expenses Account: Create a specific account in your GL for labor expenses. This might be further categorized into "Wages and Salaries," "Contractor Expenses," or "Outside Labor," depending on your needs.

Hire the Kids: The Parental Guide

Consistent Coding: Ensure all labor expenses are coded to the correct account. This consistency is key for accurate tracking and reporting.

Reporting on Payroll Expenses

Run Financial Reports to see how much you've paid in payroll expenses over the year:

1. Profit and Loss Report: Run this report to view total labor costs as part of your overall expenses.

2. Payroll Summary Report: Specifically for employee wages, taxes, deductions, and net pay.

3. Vendor Payments Report: For contractors, generate a report detailing all payments made to outside labor.

Tax Deductibility of Labor Expenses

Labor expenses are tax deductible because they are considered a necessary cost of doing business. Paying for labor, whether it's for your child, an employee, or a contractor, directly contributes to your business operations and revenue generation. These expenses reduce your taxable income, thereby potentially lowering your tax liability.

However, to ensure these deductions are legitimate, keep detailed records of all labor expenses, including timesheets, payroll records, and payment receipts. Ensure all labor practices comply with federal and state labor laws and that all tax forms and withholdings are accurate and submitted on time.

The role of a bookkeeper in managing these processes cannot be overstated. They not only ensure that your labor expenses are tracked and coded accurately but also that your business remains in good standing with tax authorities by adhering to legal and regulatory requirements. By leveraging them, you can maintain a clear picture of your labor costs and their impact on your business finances.

Hire the Kids: The Parental Guide

Hire the Kids: The Parental Guide

Section 5: The Significance of Job Descriptions

When managing a small business, clear job descriptions play a pivotal role in aligning the efforts of your team toward the collective goals of the organization. When it comes to involving your child in the business, a well-crafted job description not only legitimizes their role but also ensures their work is real, meaningful, and compliant with child labor laws.

Why Job Descriptions Are Important

Job descriptions serve as a foundational blueprint for both the employer and the employee. They clarify expectations, outline responsibilities, and set the stage for accountability and growth. For your child, a job description proves their work is not just busy work but contributes value to the business, providing them with a genuine learning and growth opportunity.

Creating a Job Description

1. **Identify the Needs of Your Business:** Determine the roles your business requires to operate efficiently. Consider what tasks your child can realistically perform based on their age, skills, and legal work restrictions.

2. **Outline Specific Responsibilities:** Clearly define what tasks the job entails. Be as detailed as possible to avoid ambiguity and ensure your child understands what is expected of them.

3. **Determine the Job's Requirements:** Note any skills or qualifications necessary to perform the job effectively. This might include basic math skills for handling transactions, communication skills for customer service roles, or technical skills for more specialized tasks.

Hire the Kids: The Parental Guide

4. **Establish Work Hours and Conditions:** Specify the hours your child will work, keeping in mind legal restrictions related to child labor. Also, describe the working conditions to ensure they are safe and appropriate.

5. **Define Performance Metrics:** Set clear, measurable goals and outcomes for the role. This will be crucial for evaluating your child's performance and providing constructive feedback.

Training Your Child on Their Duties

1. **Conduct an Orientation Session:** Introduce your child to the business environment, emphasizing the importance of their role and how it fits into the larger business operations.

2. **Review the Job Description Together:** Go through the job description in detail to ensure your child understands their responsibilities and expectations.

3. **Provide Hands-On Training:** Guide your child through the tasks they will be performing, offering practical demonstrations and opportunities for them to practice under supervision.

4. **Offer Resources for Learning:** Provide any manuals, videos, or other resources that can help your child learn about their duties and the business in general.

Supervising Your Child

1. **Set Regular Check-Ins:** Schedule daily or weekly meetings to discuss progress, address any questions, and provide feedback.

Hire the Kids: The Parental Guide

2. **Monitor Work Closely Initially**: In the early stages, observe your child's work closely to ensure they understand and can perform their duties.

3. **Gradually Increase Independence:** As your child becomes more competent, allow them more autonomy while still maintaining oversight to ensure quality and compliance.

4. **Encourage Open Communication:** Foster an environment where your child feels comfortable asking questions or expressing concerns.

Holding Your Child Accountable

1. **Refer Back to the Job Description:** Use the job description as a benchmark for evaluating your child's performance.

2. **Implement a Performance Review Process:** Conduct regular performance reviews to discuss achievements, areas for improvement, and development goals.

3. **Use Constructive Feedback:** Offer constructive and supportive feedback, focusing on specific behaviors rather than personal attributes.

4. **Reward Achievements:** Recognize and reward your child's contributions to the business, reinforcing positive behavior and encouraging continued effort and growth.

Hire the Kids: The Parental Guide

Section 6: The Zero-Based Budget Approach

Educating your child on the principles of budgeting is a vital component of their financial literacy, particularly when they start earning an income through the family business. A budget teaches children the value of money, how to manage their finances responsibly, and prepares them for financial independence. The zero-based budgeting method, in particular, is an effective tool for this purpose as it requires every dollar to be allocated to a specific purpose, ensuring thoughtful spending and saving.

Why a Budget is Important for Your Child

A budget helps your child understand the importance of living within their means, saving for the future, and making informed financial decisions. It also introduces them to the concept of financial planning and the discipline required to maintain financial health. For a child involved in a family business, learning to budget their earnings can be an invaluable lesson in money management.

How a Zero-Based Budget Works

Zero-based budgeting is a method in which every dollar of income is assigned a job, whether it's for spending, saving, or investing so that total income minus total expenses equals zero. This approach encourages meticulous financial planning and ensures that money is being used efficiently and intentionally.

Hire the Kids: The Parental Guide

Creating a Zero-Based Budget for Your Child

1. **List Monthly Income:** Start by calculating the total monthly income your child earns from the family business and any other sources.

2. **Identify and Categorize Expenses:** Help your child list all their expected monthly expenses, including savings and any discretionary spending.

3. **Assign Every Dollar a Job:** Allocate every dollar of your child's income to specific expenses, savings goals, or investment plans. Ensure that the total expenses match the total income exactly.

4. **Prioritize Savings and Investments:** Encourage your child to prioritize savings and investments, such as a savings account or a youth IRA, before allocating money to discretionary expenses.

5. **Review and Adjust Monthly:** Sit down with your child at the end of each month to review their budget, discuss what went well and what didn't, and make adjustments for the next month.

Programs for Maintaining a Zero-Based Budget

Several tools and programs can assist in creating and maintaining a zero-based budget. These include:

You Need A Budget (YNAB): This app is specifically designed around the zero-based budgeting method. It offers features that help users assign every dollar to a job and track their spending against their budget in real time.

EveryDollar: Created by personal finance expert Dave Ramsey, it follows the zero-based budgeting principle, allowing users to create customized monthly budgets and track expenses.

Hire the Kids: The Parental Guide

Excel or Google Sheets: For those who prefer a more manual approach, spreadsheet programs like Excel or Google Sheets can be used to create a custom zero-based budget. Templates are available online, or you can create one tailored to your child's needs.

By teaching your child to manage their finances through a zero-based budget, you're not only helping them understand the value of money but also equipping them with skills that will serve them throughout their life. This hands-on approach to financial education, especially when tied to their earnings from the family business, can foster a sense of responsibility, discipline, and foresight that many adults struggle to achieve.

Hire the Kids: The Parental Guide

Hire the Kids: The Parental Guide

Section 7: Your CPA and Hiring Your Child

When you decide to hire your child in your small business, it's crucial to discuss your plans with a Certified Public Accountant (CPA). This conversation ensures that you're compliant with tax laws while maximizing potential tax benefits. Here's how to approach this discussion and what to inquire about:

Discussing Your Plans

1. **Explain Your Objectives:** Clearly state why you want to hire your child, including the roles they will undertake and how it aligns with your business goals.

2. **Provide Specific Details:** Share your child's age, the nature of the work, expected hours, and how much you plan to pay them.

3. **Discuss Compliance:** Ask about the specific legal and tax requirements to ensure that hiring your child is done in full compliance with federal and state laws.

Questions for Maximizing Tax Benefits

1. **What Documentation is Needed?:** Inquire about the necessary documentation to prove your child's employment is legitimate.
2. **How Can We Optimize the Child's Income for Tax Purposes?:** Discuss the best strategies for setting your child's salary to maximize tax benefits while remaining compliant.
3. **Are There Specific Tax Forms We Should Be Aware Of?:** Understand which tax forms you'll need to file for employing your child.

Hire the Kids: The Parental Guide

4. **How Does Hiring My Child Affect My Business Deductions?:** Learn how your child's wages can be deducted as a business expense.

5. **Can My Child Contribute to a Retirement Account?:** Ask about setting up and contributing to a retirement account for your child and how it impacts taxes.

Hiring Your Child Under 18 in a Sole Proprietorship

1. **Ensure Legality of Employment:** Verify that the work is permissible for their age, complies with labor laws, and is safe.

2. **Set Up a Payroll System:** Even if informal, maintain accurate records of hours worked and payments made.

3. **Draft a Formal Job Description:** This legitimizes the employment relationship.

4. **Report Income:** Follow IRS guidelines for reporting your child's income, which may be exempt from certain taxes if under specific thresholds.

5. **Document Everything:** Keep detailed records of work performed, hours, and payments for compliance and tax purposes.

Hiring Your Child Under 18 in an LLC Owned by One Parent

1. **Check State Regulations:** Some states have specific rules for LLCs hiring family members.

2. **Formalize the Employment:** Create a job description and use a payroll system to document wages paid.

Hire the Kids: The Parental Guide

3. **Maintain Accurate Records:** Keep detailed records of work and payments.

4. **Consult Your CPA:** Determine how your child's wages will be processed through the LLC for tax purposes.

Hiring Your Child Under 18 in an S-Corp or C-Corp

1. **Understand Tax Implications:** Wages paid to children in S-Corps or C-Corps are subject to payroll taxes.

2. **Formal Employment Procedures:** Follow formal hiring processes, including job descriptions, payroll, and tax withholdings.

3. **Keep Impeccable Records**: Document all aspects of employment and compensation.

4. **Consult with Your CPA:** Review how employing your child affects corporate taxes and your child's tax obligations.

Hiring Your Child Over 18 in Your Business

1. **Evaluate Employment Terms:** Consider fair market wages for the work your child will be doing.

2. **Follow Standard Employment Practices:** This includes drafting job descriptions, setting up formal payroll, and withholding taxes.

3. **Understand Tax Implications:** Inquire with your CPA about any differences in tax treatment for adult children, including benefit eligibility and tax withholdings.

Hire the Kids: The Parental Guide

4. **Maintain Documentation:** Keep detailed employment records, including tasks performed and hours worked.

By discussing these aspects with your CPA and following the recommended steps, you can ensure that hiring your child is not only compliant but also beneficial for both your business and your child's financial future.

Hire the Kids: The Parental Guide

CHAPTER 7: Reinforcing the Rich Kid Model

Hiring your child in your small business embodies a proactive approach to financial education, offering a real-world context for lessons on money, work, and entrepreneurship. This guide has traversed the legal, financial, and practical considerations necessary to integrate your child into your business operations, from understanding child labor laws and setting up appropriate compensation to creating job descriptions and ensuring tax compliance. Each section is designed not only to comply with legal standards but also to instill valuable financial and work ethics in your child, positioning them on the "Rich Kid" path of the "Rich Kid vs. Poor Kid" model.

1. **Income vs. Allowance**: By earning through work rather than receiving an allowance, children understand the value of money and labor, fostering a work ethic and financial independence early in life.

2. **Delayed Gratification vs. Immediate Consumption**: The practice of managing their earnings teaches children the importance of budgeting, saving, and prudent financial decision-making, as opposed to the consumption-driven mindset often developed without direct involvement in financial matters.

3. **Investment Opportunities vs. Credit Dependency**: Introducing children to the concept of investment, whether through savings accounts, IRAs, or other vehicles, cultivates an understanding of growth and future planning, steering them away from financial dependency and towards autonomy.

4. **Skill Development & Entrepreneurship vs. Recreation & Education**: Active participation in a family business enriches

Hire the Kids: The Parental Guide

children with practical skills and entrepreneurial insights, providing a solid foundation for personal and professional development beyond the classroom or recreational activities.

Hire the Kids: The Parental Guide

The Benefits of Raising a "Rich Kid"

Bringing the "Rich Kid" model into your family business is one of the best investments you can make in your child's future. In this context, being a "Rich Kid" isn't about being born with a silver spoon or having an easy life handed to them. It's about something much deeper and more meaningful. A "Rich Kid" is a child who rolls up their sleeves and dives into the family business, not just as a bystander but as a real employee earning their keep. This hands-on experience gives them a head start in understanding how the world of finance and business works, setting them up with skills and knowledge that are hard to come by at such a young age.

The term "Rich Kid" takes on a whole new meaning here. It's about giving your child more than just financial wealth—it's about equipping them with the tools to build their own future. By working in the family business, these kids learn what it means to manage money, solve problems, and think like an entrepreneur. They're not just learning to handle wealth; they're learning to create it. This approach instills a sense of financial independence and business savvy that can shape their lives for years to come, helping to build a legacy that's not just about having money but about knowing how to make it grow.

Through this model, you're not just preparing them for the next big challenge; you're teaching them how to thrive in a world that's constantly changing. They learn early on that success doesn't come from entitlement but from hard work, creativity, and the ability to adapt. By being actively involved in the family business, they gain a perspective that few of their peers have—a real understanding of what it takes to run a business, make smart decisions, and build something that lasts.

Gaining Practical Experience Early

One of the biggest advantages of the "Rich Kid" model is the practical experience your child gains from a young age. While many of their peers might only learn about business concepts in a classroom setting, your child gets to see how these concepts play out in the real world. They get a front-row seat to the day-to-day operations of the business, learning everything from customer service to inventory management and financial planning. This kind of experience is invaluable because it teaches them how businesses work from the ground up.

Having a child involved in the business from an early age also means they learn to appreciate the hard work and dedication that goes into making a business successful. They see firsthand the challenges you face, whether it's dealing with difficult customers, managing cash flow, or navigating market fluctuations. These experiences teach them resilience and problem-solving skills that are crucial in any career path they choose to pursue later on. It also shows them that success isn't something that happens overnight but is the result of consistent effort and smart decision-making.

Building Financial Literacy

Another significant benefit of the "Rich Kid" model is the early financial literacy it fosters. When kids are involved in a family business, they learn about money management in a very real and tangible way. They see how revenues come in, how expenses are paid, and how profits are calculated. This practical education goes far beyond what they might learn in a typical economics class. They learn the importance of budgeting, saving, and investing—skills that will serve them well throughout their lives.

As they get older, you can gradually introduce them to more complex financial concepts. You might start by teaching them how to balance the books or manage payroll. Over time, they can learn about things like cash flow management, tax planning, and financial forecasting. These are skills that will not only help them if they decide to run their own business one day but also give them a leg up in personal financial management, making them more financially independent and secure.

Developing a Strong Work Ethic

There's something to be said about the work ethic that comes from growing up in a family business. When children see their parents

Hire the Kids: The Parental Guide

working hard and dedicating themselves to building something meaningful, it sets a powerful example. It teaches them the value of hard work, commitment, and perseverance. They learn that in business, as in life, there are no shortcuts to success.

By working in the family business, kids also learn about the importance of accountability and responsibility. They see that every member of the team has a role to play and that the success of the business depends on everyone doing their part. When they have a job to do, they learn to take it seriously, knowing that their efforts have a direct impact on the business's bottom line. This sense of responsibility can translate into other areas of their life, from their studies to their personal relationships.

Encouraging an Entrepreneurial Mindset

One of the most valuable aspects of the "Rich Kid" model is how it encourages an entrepreneurial mindset. When kids grow up around business, they learn to think like entrepreneurs. They see opportunities where others see obstacles, and they learn to be creative in solving problems. They become comfortable with taking calculated risks and are more likely to think outside the box.

This entrepreneurial spirit can be incredibly empowering. It teaches children that they have the ability to shape their own futures and that they don't have to follow a conventional path if they don't want to. Whether they decide to take over the family business, start their own venture, or pursue a career in another field, the skills and mindset they develop from this experience will give them a significant advantage.

Learning the Value of Teamwork

Running a family business is often a team effort, and involving your child in the business gives them a chance to learn the value of teamwork. They see how different roles and responsibilities come together to achieve a common goal. They learn to communicate effectively, collaborate with others, and understand the importance of each team member's contribution.

Hire the Kids: The Parental Guide

Teamwork is a skill that is valuable in every aspect of life. By learning to work well with others in a business setting, children also develop empathy, listening skills, and the ability to compromise. These skills will serve them well not only in their future careers but also in their personal relationships and community involvement.

Preparing for the Future

Perhaps one of the most compelling reasons to implement the "Rich Kid" model is the preparation it provides for the future. By involving your child in the family business, you're giving them a head start in life. They gain a wealth of knowledge and experience that can help them make informed decisions about their education and career paths. They also develop a strong sense of self-confidence and independence, knowing that they have the skills and capabilities to succeed in whatever they choose to do.

In a world that's constantly changing, having a solid foundation in business and finance can provide a significant advantage. The "Rich Kid" model helps children develop adaptability and resilience, which are essential traits in today's fast-paced world. Whether they decide to continue in the family business or forge their own path, they'll have the tools and mindset needed to navigate the challenges and opportunities that come their way.

Creating a Legacy

Finally, the "Rich Kid" model is about more than just the here and now—it's about creating a lasting legacy. By teaching your child the ins and outs of the family business, you're not only passing on valuable skills but also instilling a sense of pride and ownership. They learn about the history of the business, the values that have driven its success, and the importance of maintaining those values in the future.

This sense of legacy is powerful. It gives children a deeper understanding of where they come from and what they are a part of. It also encourages them to think about what kind of legacy they want to leave behind. By involving them in the family business, you're giving them the opportunity to contribute to something bigger than

Hire the Kids: The Parental Guide

themselves, something that can be passed down through generations.

Measuring the "Rich Kid" Model for Your Child

Figuring out whether the "Rich Kid" model is really making a difference in your child's development takes a bit of time and observation. It's not just about them earning a wage or helping out in the family business; it's about looking deeper into how these experiences are shaping them into well-rounded, financially savvy individuals. Let's break down some ways you can measure this impact and see if it's setting your child up for future success.

First off, one of the main goals of the "Rich Kid" model is to boost your child's financial know-how. You want to see if they're learning how to handle money wisely. Start by checking out their ability to create and stick to a budget. Sit down with them every so often and go over their budget plans. Compare what they thought they'd spend with what they actually spent. This isn't about nitpicking but about guiding them to understand where their money goes. Keep an eye on their saving habits, too. Are they setting aside a portion of their earnings? Do they grasp the basics of investing, like understanding what interest rates are, how loans work, or what investment risks mean? Having casual conversations about these topics or throwing in a few informal quizzes can give you a good sense of how much they're picking up.

Beyond financial literacy, another big area to focus on is their work ethic and sense of responsibility. Now, this can be a bit more subjective, but there are definitely some signs to look for. See if your child is reliable in getting their tasks done on time and doing them well. Consistency here is key—if they're regularly hitting the mark, that's a good sign they're developing a strong work ethic. Pay attention to whether they're taking initiative. Do they come up with suggestions for improvements or offer to take on extra tasks without being asked? That's them showing they're engaged and willing to go above and beyond. And when you give them feedback, how do they handle it? If they're open to learning from their mistakes and are

Hire the Kids: The Parental Guide

keen on improving, that's a sure sign they're developing a good sense of responsibility.

The skills they're learning while working in the family business are also worth tracking. This doesn't just mean the hard skills, like becoming proficient in bookkeeping, customer service, or managing social media. Those are important, no doubt, and you can easily measure progress in these areas through regular performance reviews. But don't overlook the soft skills—things like communication, teamwork, and problem-solving. These are a bit harder to quantify, but you can get a sense of how they're developing through feedback from colleagues or even self-assessment surveys.

Encouraging an entrepreneurial mindset is another key aspect of the "Rich Kid" model. This means nurturing their creativity, innovation, and ability to think strategically. Look at how involved they are in new projects or business ideas. Are they actively participating in brainstorming sessions? Are they coming up with new ideas or suggesting ways to improve existing processes? Keep track of these contributions and any actions that result from their suggestions. This not only provides concrete evidence of their entrepreneurial spirit but also helps them see the impact of their contributions. Talk with them about how they approach risk-taking and decision-making in the business. Understanding their thought process can give you insights into how they're growing in this area.

It's also crucial to make sure your child is keeping a healthy balance between work, school, and their personal life. After all, the goal isn't to turn them into little workaholics. Keep an eye on their grades and school performance to ensure their work in the business isn't negatively affecting their education. Check if they're managing their time well and balancing their work duties, school responsibilities, and downtime. A well-organized schedule that they stick to is a good sign they're managing things effectively. Regular check-ins can help you gauge how they're feeling and whether they're handling everything without feeling overwhelmed.

Lastly, think about the long-term impact of these experiences on their future. What kind of career aspirations do they have? Are they

Hire the Kids: The Parental Guide

leaning more toward entrepreneurship or business-related fields? Look at how their experience in the family business is helping them with college admissions or scholarships. Are they able to manage their finances independently as they grow older? This includes budgeting, saving, investing, and making smart financial choices. These are all signs that the "Rich Kid" model is setting them up for success in adulthood.

By regularly evaluating these areas, you can get a clear picture of how the "Rich Kid" model is impacting your child's development. This ongoing assessment ensures that the lessons and experiences they gain while working in the family business translate into valuable skills and a solid foundation for their future.

Wearing Two Hats: Being Both Parent and Boss

If you're a small business owner thinking about hiring your kid, you're about to step into a whole new world where you're not just wearing one hat but two. You're still their parent, but now you're also their boss. And let's be honest—it's a balancing act. It's hard enough running a business, but adding in the dynamics of family can make things get complicated really fast. Still, if you handle it right, bringing your child into the family business can strengthen both your bond and your bottom line.

The key is to set clear boundaries right from the get-go. You've got to make sure your child knows what's expected of them, just like you would with any other employee. Spell out their role, their duties, their hours—everything. It might feel a little strange to hand your kid a job description, but trust me, this sets the stage for a professional working relationship and makes sure there are no misunderstandings down the road.

Now, here's where it can get a bit tricky. When you're their parent at home and their boss at work, those lines can blur pretty easily. So, it's crucial to keep family stuff separate from business matters. When you're at the dinner table, be a family. Leave the work talk at the office. This way, both you and your child can switch gears and fully engage in whatever role you're playing at the moment.

Hire the Kids: The Parental Guide

One practical way to keep things on track is to have regular check-ins or meetings just for business. During these sessions, treat your child like any other employee. Talk about their performance, give them feedback, and set goals. This not only helps them see their place in the business but also reinforces that they're an important part of the team.

But let's not forget—you're still their parent. Don't lose the warmth and encouragement that comes naturally in that role. Recognize their hard work and celebrate their successes, whether they've nailed a project or just had a really great week. A little positive reinforcement goes a long way in building confidence and motivating them to keep pushing forward.

Inevitably, there are going to be bumps in the road. Disagreements are part of any business, but when it's your kid, it can feel a lot more personal. When conflicts arise, deal with them professionally. Listen to their side, give constructive feedback, and work together to find a solution. This approach not only keeps the peace but also teaches your child valuable skills in conflict resolution.

Balancing these roles as a parent and boss is no cakewalk, but with a little planning and a lot of communication, it can be incredibly rewarding. By setting boundaries, keeping family and business matters separate, and treating your child like a valued member of the team, you're helping them develop the skills and work ethic they need to succeed. And that, right there, is what the "Rich Kid" model is all about.

Keep Learning: Building a Growth Mindset

As a parent and a business owner, one of the best things you can teach your child is the value of a growth mindset. This is all about encouraging them to see challenges as opportunities, to learn from mistakes, and to never stop improving. When you're looking to reinforce the "Rich Kid" model, fostering this mindset is key. It's not just about teaching them to work hard—it's about helping them learn to think creatively, adapt to change, and see every experience as a chance to grow.

Hire the Kids: The Parental Guide

The business world is always changing. New technologies pop up, markets shift, and customer tastes evolve. If you want your kid to thrive in this environment, you've got to help them learn to roll with the punches. Encourage them to take on new projects or responsibilities that push them out of their comfort zone. Maybe they can learn a new software program, lead a team project, or handle some customer service. Whatever it is, these experiences will help them build new skills and gain confidence.

And when they stumble—and they will—remind them that it's all part of the process. Mistakes aren't failures; they're learning opportunities. The key is to reflect on what went wrong and figure out how to do better next time. This kind of thinking will help them become more resilient and better equipped to handle whatever comes their way.

Lead by example. Share your own experiences with them. Talk about the mistakes you've made in your business, what you learned from them, and how those lessons helped you improve. This shows your child that everyone, no matter how experienced, is always learning and growing.

Help your child set goals for both their personal and professional development. These could be anything from mastering a particular skill to reading a few books on business or self-improvement each year. Setting and working toward these goals teaches them the value of continuous learning and self-betterment. And don't forget to celebrate their achievements along the way, no matter how small. Acknowledging their efforts keeps them motivated and eager to keep pushing themselves.

Also, encourage them to explore interests outside of work. Hobbies and activities like playing an instrument, learning a new language, or playing sports can challenge them in different ways and help them build a well-rounded set of skills. Plus, it keeps life interesting!

In the end, fostering a growth mindset in your child is about instilling a love of learning and a belief in their ability to improve. By encouraging them to embrace challenges, learn from mistakes, and

Hire the Kids: The Parental Guide

constantly seek new opportunities for growth, you're setting them up for success—not just in the family business, but in life. This approach is at the heart of the "Rich Kid" model, helping your child develop the mindset, skills, and resilience they need to thrive no matter what the future holds.

Why Hiring Your Kid is the Best Move

Deciding to hire your child to work in your small business isn't just about adding another set of hands to the team—it's about opening up a whole world of opportunities for them. It's the real-life application of what we've been calling the "Rich Kid" model, and it's more than just giving them a job. It's about showing them the ropes, teaching them the value of hard work, and giving them a crash course in how money really works.

Throughout this book, we've talked about how this isn't just employment; it's a full-on learning experience that sets your child up with the skills they need to succeed on their own. They're not just filling a role; they're getting a head start on learning what it means to take responsibility, make smart decisions, and think like an entrepreneur. And let's face it, that's something you can't always teach in school.

This whole idea of the "Rich Kid" isn't about wealth in the way most people think. It's not about being born into money or having an easy ride. It's about raising kids who understand what it takes to build something from the ground up and who aren't afraid to roll up their sleeves and get their hands dirty. It's about showing them that wealth isn't just about having money—it's about knowing how to make it, manage it, and grow it.

By bringing your child into the family business, you're giving them a front-row seat to see how things work in the real world. They're learning about everything from customer service to managing the books to dealing with the ups and downs that come with running a business. These lessons aren't just important—they're invaluable. They're learning skills they'll carry with them for the rest of their lives, skills that will help them in whatever path they choose, whether

Hire the Kids: The Parental Guide

that's taking over the family business, starting their own venture, or going in a completely different direction.

And it's not just about work skills. You're also teaching them life skills. They're learning to be dependable, to show up on time, to take pride in their work, and to understand that being part of a team means sometimes putting the needs of the business ahead of their own. They're learning that success doesn't come easy and that it's okay to make mistakes as long as you learn from them and keep moving forward.

When you hire your kid, you're making an investment in their future. You're betting on their potential and showing them that you believe in what they can do. You're not just hiring an employee; you're mentoring a future leader, someone who can think critically, adapt to changes, and face challenges head-on. That's what the "Rich Kid vs. Poor Kid" model is all about—giving kids the tools and mindset they need to be successful, no matter what the future holds.

At the end of the day, this is about more than just building wealth. It's about creating opportunities, building character, and laying the groundwork for a legacy that can be passed down through generations. It's about raising kids who aren't just ready to manage what's handed to them but are equipped to build their own future.

By bringing them into the business, you're doing more than just giving them a job. You're teaching them how to think like an entrepreneur, how to make smart financial decisions, and how to see opportunities where others might only see challenges. They're learning to be self-sufficient, to take initiative, and to understand the value of a hard day's work.

This model is about preparing them for the real world, giving them a head start on building a life that's not only successful but meaningful. It's about teaching them that wealth isn't just about what you have but about what you do with what you've got.

So, as you wrap up this journey and start thinking about how to put these ideas into action, remember this: hiring your child isn't just about what they can do for your business. It's about what this

Hire the Kids: The Parental Guide

experience can do for them. It's about setting them up with the skills, knowledge, and mindset they need to go out and create their own success story. It's about building a legacy that will last far beyond the time they spend working in the family business.

You're not just teaching them to follow in your footsteps—you're giving them the foundation they need to carve out their own path. And that, in the end, is the best gift you can give. So go ahead, take the leap. Bring them into the fold. Show them what it means to be a "Rich Kid," not just in terms of money, but in terms of character, knowledge, and resilience. Because in the grand scheme of things, that's what really matters. That's the legacy worth leaving behind.

Hire the Kids: The Parental Guide

Hire the Kids: The Parental Guide

"Ready to embark on a transformative journey that bridges the gap between family and business? Visit our website at WWW.HIRETHEKIDS.COM to delve deeper into 'HIRE THE KIDS: The Parental Journey.' Discover more enriching content, gain exclusive insights, and access additional resources that will guide you in integrating your children into your business while building a legacy. Don't miss out on the opportunity to transform your family's future. Click now to explore and take the first step towards a successful, family-inclusive entrepreneurial journey!"

www.ingramcontent.com/pod-product-compliance
Lightning Source LLC
Chambersburg PA
CBHW060845050426
42453CB00008B/843